Volcanoes
A Beginner's Guide

ONEWORLD BEGINNER'S GUIDES combine an original, inventive, and engaging approach with expert analysis on subjects ranging from art and history to religion and politics, and everything in between. Innovative and affordable, books in the series are perfect for anyone curious about the way the world works and the big ideas of our time.

Beginners
GUIDES

Volcanoes
A Beginner's Guide

Rosaly Lopes

ONEWORLD
OXFORD

A Oneworld Book

Published by Oneworld Publications 2010

Copyright © Rosaly Lopes 2010

The moral right of Rosaly Lopes to be identified as the Author
of this work has been asserted by her in accordance with the
Copyright, Designs and Patents Act 1988

All rights reserved
Copyright under Berne Convention
A CIP record for this title is available from the British Library

ISBN 978-1-85168-725-1

Typeset by Glyph International
Cover design by vaguelymemorable.com
Printed and bound by
Bell & Bain Ltd., Glasgow

Oneworld Publications
185 Banbury Road, Oxford, OX2 7AR, England

Learn more about Oneworld. Join our mailing list
to find out about our latest titles and special offers at:
www.oneworld-publications.com

Mixed Sources

Product group from well-managed
forests and other controlled sources
www.fsc.org   Cert no. TT-COC-002769
© 1996 Forest Stewardship Council

This book is dedicated to the explorer and adventurer Ralph B White (1941–2008)

Contents

Acknowledgments

Many colleagues provided valuable input and illustrations for this book. I am particularly grateful to Scott Rowland who has generously allowed me to use many of his beautiful photographs, to Charlie Bluehawk who drafted some of the diagrams and to Chuck Wood who reviewed the manuscript draft and made excellent suggestions. My editors at Oneworld have guided this book to completion; my special thanks to Fiona Slater, Marsha Filion and Victoria Roddam.

Illustrations

Colour plates

1

What are volcanoes?

What is your idea of a volcano? The image that probably comes to mind is a violent, angry mountain, spewing out black clouds of ash and rivers of red-hot lava, burning villages and causing devastation and tragedy. We think of Vesuvius in Ancient Roman times and its destruction of the libidinous Pompeii; we think of the eruption of Krakatoa in the nineteenth century and its catastrophic tsunami that took countless lives.

Every now and then, the media focuses on a volcano that is at the very least worrying local people and sometimes playing downright havoc with their lives. In 2010, the Eyjafjallajökull volcano in Iceland demonstrated just how disruptive volcanic eruptions can be. Although its eruption was small compared to eruptions such as that of Pinatubo in 1991, its ash cloud, rising up to nine kilometers high, blew over Europe, stopping air traffic for several days. Thousands of travellers were stranded and the economic impact was felt world-wide.

All these images are true some of the time but, in reality, volcanoes come with different shapes, sizes and temperaments. It is fascinating to study what causes these differences and understand that, while some generalisations are possible, each volcano has its distinct quirks, just like people. We could also compare volcanoes to cats: with few exceptions, they spend most of their lives asleep.

We will start our fascinating journey of understanding volcanoes on Earth, travelling from its beginnings to the evolution of its many cultures, with their diverse explanations of what volcanoes are and why they erupt. We will then travel on to the other planets of our solar system: volcanoes are fundamental to the formation of planets and many types exist, from the rampant, hot volcanic activity of Jupiter's moon Io to the cold, exotic cryovolcanism (eruptions consisting mostly of liquid water from the interior of icy moons) in the outer solar system.

What, exactly, is a volcano?

A volcano is an opening on the surface of a planet from which magma and/or magmatic gas emerges. Magma is molten rock, containing dissolved gases and crystals; it originates in the mantle, which typically lies eighty to one hundred kilometers below the planetary surface. When a volcano erupts, magma emerges in one or more forms: continuous lava flows, fragments varying in size from boulders to ash or rapidly flowing currents of hot gas and rock fragments. The erupting lava and gases build up around the opening (or vent) to form the volcano.

The landform created could be a field of lava, a cone or, eventually, a mountain. Sometimes lava pours out onto the surface without explosions and no built-up landform is discernible. You can walk for miles over the lava fields of the Krafla volcano in Iceland without climbing a mountain or even a sizeable hill: Krafla's lavas pour out of great fissures and the volcano is all around you. On other volcanoes, the exploded fragments of lava that land close to the vent build relatively small but steep-sided cones, such as the cones of Stromboli in the Aeolian Islands and Sunset Crater in Arizona, USA. The combination of lava flows and explosive eruptions over long periods builds the tallest volcanoes, such as Mount Fuji in Japan, a volcano that, for many, is the classic, with its convex-upward shape and serene, snow-capped summit.

On Earth, the type and shape of a volcano is largely dependent on its tectonic setting, that is, where it is located relative to the tectonic plates. However, before we go into that, let's go back in time and history to remind ourselves how the inhabitants of many places and of many cultures co-existed with volcanoes and tried to understand their nature.

Volcanoes and human history

People and volcanoes have a turbulent history. Mary Leakey's discovery, in 1978, of hominid (*Australopithecus*) footprints some 3.7 million years old impressed on a volcanic ash deposit at Laetoli in Tanzania is a stunning example of how long this fragile co-existence has lasted. During and following an eruption, the effects of volcanic ash are devastating but, as the years pass, it contributes to the soil's fertility. People have long farmed the rich land on the slopes of dormant volcanoes, perhaps for many years, before a catastrophic event brought their towns, their farms and even their lives to an unfortunate end.

The earliest known tools made by humans were made from volcanic stone. Implements made from lava about 2.5 million years old were found at Lokalalei, on the shores of Lake Turkana in northern Kenya. Obsidian, a black volcanic glass familiar to many of us, was prized in the Palaeolithic (Stone) Age for its hardness, durability and ability to split cleanly. It can be made into needle-sharp points and blades, including the familiar arrow-heads. Our ancestors used volcanic pumice and ash to make cement – the ash, when mixed with lime, produces a durable, water-resistant cement that has been used since Ancient Roman times. On a visit to the Greek volcanic island of Santorini, I learnt that pumice deposited by its Minoan eruption was used in the construction of the Suez Canal. Pumice quarries are still being worked in many parts of the world; many of us have a piece of a volcano in our bathrooms.

Another prized product of volcanoes is sulphur, once known as brimstone (volcanoes are notoriously the embodiment of Hell on Earth). Sulphur burns with a strange, sputtering flame and produces the eye-stinging gas, sulphur dioxide, used to fumigate houses to kill insects or to bleach wool. Homer refers to sulphur being used this way; in ancient Greece, Egypt and Rome it was also believed to have medicinal purposes. Even today, in some volcanic 'spa' areas, such as the island of Vulcano in Italy, the dubious medicinal uses of volcanic mud and fumes are touted as curative. The war-mongering Romans used a mixture containing sulphur as the first incendiary weapon, but not until the thirteenth century was sulphur's great potential in warfare discovered by the Chinese, as a key ingredient in gunpowder. When the knowledge of gunpowder came to Europe in the early fourteenth century its impact was huge. Knights in shining armour were no match for the explosive mixture and the character of war changed forever. Centuries later, gunpowder helped take the Americas from their native tribes. When, in Mexico, Hernando Cortés found himself short of sulphur to make gunpowder, he sent some of his loyal soldiers into the crater of the active Popocatepetl volcano to collect some. The soldiers were successful, even though the volcano exploded during their mission.

Volcanoes also yield more traditional riches – diamonds and gold are found in the eroded roots of ancient volcanoes – but, in some places, volcanoes are precious because they make life better or even possible. From the fertile slopes of Vesuvius, where grapes have been cultivated for centuries, to geothermal heat sources in Iceland, volcanoes have a profound influence on our lives and culture. While it is true that volcanoes can kill, the death toll from volcanic eruptions is usually low compared to that from other natural disasters like floods, hurricanes and earthquakes. As our knowledge of how volcanoes work increases, we are increasingly able to predict when a particular volcano is likely to erupt. To the people living in the shadow of an active volcano, this knowledge is invaluable. This is why, for many centuries, humans have attempted to answer the most important question in volcanology: why do volcanoes erupt?

Myth and history

While some explained volcanic fury in the terms they understood best – gods and goddesses – others attempted to put forward scientific explanations for the fire from within the Earth. The first interpretations we know of are from the Ancient Greek philosophers. In the fifth century BCE, Anaxagoras proposed that volcanic eruptions were caused by great winds within the Earth, blowing through narrow passages. He explained the melting of rocks as being caused by friction of these winds buffeting against rocks in the passages. This explanation, later adopted by Aristotle, was remarkably long-lived, surviving in one form or another until the Middle Ages. In Ancient Rome, the philosopher Seneca proposed an alternative explanation; that volcanoes were giant furnaces in which coal, bitumen and sulphur were burning. This view survived for many centuries.

HEPHAESTUS AND VULCAN

People living alongside volcanoes have attempted to explain the rumblings, shaking and fiery eruptions in many ways. To the Greeks, the god of fire, Hephaestus (called Vulcan by the Romans), lived beneath Etna in Sicily. Working beside his helpers, the terrifying single-eyed giant Cyclops, Hephaestus hammered on his anvil, forging thunderbolts for Jupiter. Other legends set Hephaestus's forge beneath the island of Vulcano in the Aeolian archipelago, which gave its name to all volcanoes.

In the seventeenth century, the French scientist and mathematician, René Descartes, proposed that the Earth had been a star and volcanic eruptions were caused by the intense heat still trapped within our planet. In the eighteenth century, basaltic rocks were accepted as having been created by ancient volcanic eruptions, resulting in the recognition of ancient volcanic rocks from various places around the world. Historically, this was the victory of the Plutonists, who held that rocks were formed in volcanic eruptions, over the Neptunists, who believed that rocks formed from the crystallisation of minerals in the early Earth's oceans. Thus, igneous petrology – the study of the melting and crystallisation of volcanic rocks – began in earnest.

In the nineteenth century volcanology made a significant leap forward, when the pioneering geophysicists George Poulett Scrope and William Hopkins discovered that rocks melt without addition of heat, if they move upwards towards the Earth's surface, where the pressure is lower. Hence there was no need for a 'furnace' or other heat to melt the rocks. However, what made rocks move upwards? An explanation had been proposed in the eighteenth century by Count Rumford, who suggested that there were convective currents within the Earth. These large-scale, very slow currents can move rocks up, which then, as Scrope and Hopkins's findings explained, melt because of the decrease in pressure. In the early twentieth century, the heat source driving these currents was discovered to be caused by the radioactive decay of certain elements within the Earth. The early part of the twentieth century also saw the work of Arthur Holmes, who brought together these ideas and laid the foundation for the theory of plate tectonics. Since then, we have made ever-greater advances, but volcanology still presents many questions. Although we have come a long way from the days of appeasing the gods, we still have much to learn about what makes volcanoes erupt.

Where are volcanoes found?

Active volcanoes are found on every one of the Earth's continents, even Antarctica. About 600 continental volcanoes are considered active – meaning that they have erupted within the last 10,000 years – but there are many more under the sea.

The majority of the Earth's volcanoes are submarine, although many people have heard little about these underwater volcanoes, probably because, when they erupt, they kill only fish. History and journalists tend to favour human catastrophes.

Whether they are underwater or on land, volcanoes don't randomly pop up here or there. The location of volcanoes is controlled by plate tectonics; with rare exceptions, the Earth's volcanoes sprout at plate boundaries, concentrated in narrow chains that follow the boundaries (see Figure 1), where over ninety-four per cent of historic eruptions have occurred. It is not a coincidence that most earthquakes occur along the same boundaries, where the Earth's plates are spreading apart (the mid-oceanic ridges) or being pushed together (subduction zones).

The Earth's crust is made up of plates that fit together like a giant jigsaw puzzle. Beneath the plates lies the mantle, covering the planet's hot interior. Heat from the deep interior causes a circulation in the solid mantle, which flows very slowly, like ice in a glacier. Rock flowing upwards within the mantle eventually

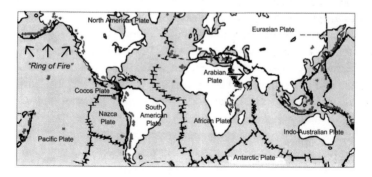

Figure 1 The Earth's tectonic plates. Arrows show direction of movement of plates. Most of the Earth's volcanoes are located at plate margins, which are either divergent (where they are spreading) or convergent (where subduction zones are located). (Modified from Decker and Decker, 1991.)

reaches a level, at about seventy kilometres beneath the surface, where the temperature is high enough and the pressure low enough for some of the rock to melt. The molten rock in turn rises upwards, because it is less dense than the surrounding solid rock. This molten rock – magma – rises through zones of weaknesses in the crust. These zones of weakness are the plate boundaries; hence magma most often reaches the surface along the mid-oceanic ridges and subduction zones. There are some exceptions; volcanoes can also emerge in the middle of plates. These are known as intracontinental volcanism and hot spot volcanism. It is important to understand each of these different zones, because where the magma comes up – along mid-oceanic ridges, subduction zones, in intracontinental regions or in hot spots – has a big effect on the type of volcano and eruption.

Mid-oceanic ridges

What do cold, barren Iceland and the sunny Canary Islands have in common? They are all volcanic islands formed by the activity of the Mid-Atlantic Ridge. Most of the volcanoes along the ridge are under water but here and there they poke through the ocean's surface to construct islands. At the southern end is the uninhabited Bouvet Island, which belongs to Norway, which also owns the equally inhospitable Jan Mayen Island at the northern end of the chain. In between lie the volcanic paradise of Iceland, one of the best places on Earth to see and study volcanoes, and the lovely Canaries, Azores and Cape Verde islands. A few less-visited places mark the ridge above water, including the island of Santa Helena, famous as Napoleon's last home. Beneath the water lies another world of volcanoes, in some ways much more fantastic.

Volcanoes along the Mid-Atlantic Ridge are created because two tectonic plates (the Eurasian Plate and North American Plate) are spreading apart, allowing magma to erupt and to create new crust. When eruptions occur in the same place for long

ATLANTIS

One of the greatest eruptions in history, Santorini, which occurred some time between 1650 and 1600 BCE, has been blamed for many things, from the end of Minoan civilisation to the Biblical plagues of Egypt. It may even have inspired the enduring myth of Atlantis. The Greek philosopher Plato wrote of the sudden disappearance of a vast island and its people 'in a single day and night'.

periods of time, mountains build from the bottom of the sea and, eventually, a new island is created. Magma erupting on the ocean floor pours out relatively gently, as vast amounts of basaltic lava. Underwater volcanoes also create some rather impressive expressions called 'chimneys' or 'smokers', formed when superheated water comes through the crust into the cold ocean floor. The superheated water contains dissolved minerals, particularly sulphides (chemical compounds containing sulphur), and flows out at several metres per second. When the hot water meets the cold ocean water, the minerals precipitate out, causing the 'smoke'. Black smokers have temperatures of up to 400°C, while white smokers are somewhat cooler. On average, black smokers are found around 2,100 metres below the ocean's surface. The discovery of these smokers helped to confirm the theory of plate tectonics.

Subduction zones

If the Earth's plates are spreading apart in mid-oceanic ridges, they must be either destroyed or pushed back down elsewhere. This happens at the subduction zones, where oceanic crust, which is denser than continental crust, is pushed beneath the continental crust and, together with sediments and water, carried down a steep slope into the mantle. Subduction zones are found where oceanic and continental plates are pushed against one another; for example, along the western coast of the Americas, where we find volcanoes from Alaska down to southern Chile. The heat of subduction causes parts of both the oceanic and continental plates to melt. Molten rock is less dense than solid rock, so the molten rock rises towards the surface. These magmas tend to have different compositions to the basalts that erupt from mid-ocean ridges; we can think of them as 'recycled', since they are produced by melting of the crust and sediments. Geologists define these magmas as being more 'evolved' than basalt. These more evolved magmas tend to make more explosive eruptions; some of the most explosive and potentially dangerous volcanoes in the world are found in subduction zones. The 'Ring of Fire' around the Pacific Ocean is a good example; some of the most explosive volcanoes on Earth, such as Krakatoa and Tambora, in Indonesia, lie along the Ring of Fire.

When two oceanic plates collide and one plate subducts back into the mantle, an 'island arc' is created. Island chains of active volcanoes, such as the Lesser Antilles in the Caribbean, where the notorious Mount Pelée in Martinique is located, form atop these zones. One island arc volcano that has been very active recently is Soufrière Hills on the Caribbean island of Montserrat; this island has been devastated by a long-running eruption that started in 1995 and has lasted over a decade.

Hot spots

Some volcanoes exist away from plate boundaries. A particularly good example of such 'hot spot' volcanism is Hawaii, an island chain created by volcanic eruptions in the middle of the Pacific Plate. Hot spots are thought to be long-lived mantle plumes, upwellings of abnormally hot rock from deep within the Earth's mantle, originating hundreds or even over one thousand kilometres down, which feed magma through either an oceanic or a continental plate, away from plate boundaries.

PELE

One of the best-known volcano gods is Pele, the Hawaiian goddess of volcanoes. A significant number of Hawaiians still worship Pele and many claim to have seen her. The early Polynesians who came to Hawaii showed a surprising amount of understanding of the way volcanism in the islands work, explaining it in terms of the wanderings of Pele. The volcanoes making up the Hawaiian chain become progressively younger (and more active) towards the south-eastern end of the chain; early Hawaiians attributed this progression to Pele's search for a home, in a constant battle with her elder sister, Na-maka-o-Kaha'i, the goddess of sea and water. Pele was finally allowed to make her home in Kilauea, currently the most active of the Hawaiian volcanoes.

The first eruption from a hot spot is thought to be the largest, pouring out enormous quantities of basaltic lava. If the hot spot erupts through a continental plate, hot, runny basaltic lava flows onto the surface. All land eruptions from hot spots happened millions of years ago, forming large plains of 'flood basalts' such as the Columbia River basalts in the western USA and the Giant's Causeway in Ireland. When hot spots erupt through an oceanic plate, over millions of years they build volcanoes that eventually poke through the ocean's surface as islands. Measured from ocean floor to tip, these volcanoes are the largest mountains on Earth. All the Hawaiian islands have been formed by a single hot spot that has remained active for at least the last seventy million years. However, although the hot spot is stationary, the Pacific Plate has moved north–west, so instead of one volcano, a chain has emerged. The volcanoes at the north–western end of the chain are dead, because they are no longer being fed by the hot spot. Kilauea, at the south-eastern end of the chain, is currently the most active, but eventually a new volcano will claim that title; the Loihi volcano is slowly being built up and, one day – at least 10,000 years from now – will poke through the ocean's surface to become the newest piece of the Hawaiian paradise.

Intracontinental volcanism

This is the most complex type, because it is something of a mixed bag. The eruptions occur away from plate margins and can be the result either of a hot spot or of rifting of the crust. The magma comes up through continental rather than oceanic crust, to erupt at the surface. In some places, such as Arizona and California in the western USA, the local crust is particularly thin, which facilitates the eruption of magma at the surface. The East African Rift Valley is a dramatic example of intracontinental volcanism; its huge gash extends from the Red Sea, through Ethiopia, down to Mozambique. Kilimanjaro, the highest peak in Africa and the continent's most famous volcano, is a result of volcanism on the rift; other gorgeous volcanoes include Erta Ale in Ethiopia and Ol Doinyo Lengai in Tanzania.

2

How volcanoes erupt

The basic principles of how volcanoes erupt are the same wherever they are found. Because magma is less dense than solid rock, it is able to rise up from the mantle along plate boundaries and other zones of weakness in the crust. Most volcanoes have a magma chamber beneath them; some lie just a few kilometres under the surface, others are tens of kilometres deep. Magma may stay in the chamber for years until pressure in the magma chamber builds, generated by an influx of new magma into the chamber, causing the rock to fracture and magma to be released. The fracturing triggers earthquakes, which often signal that an eruption is about to happen.

Why do some volcanoes erupt with a big bang while others have gentle effusions of lava flows? The key factor is the gases dissolved in the magma, which include water, carbon dioxide and sulphur dioxide, amongst others. Volcanoes are often topped by a plume of gas (mostly steam) and clothed in a pungent stench of rotten eggs from the sulphurous gases. As the magma rises towards the surface, the temperature and pressure decrease, making it possible for the gases to escape (imagine what happens when you take the top off a can of fizzy drink or, for more fun, a bottle of champagne!).

The way the gases come out of the magma determines the explosivity of an eruption; if the magma contains gases and is very fluid, like Hawaiian basalts, the gases can bubble out, frequently forming 'fire fountains' (also called lava fountains). However, if the magma is gas-rich and syrupy (viscous), the gases cannot escape easily and will eventually explode out, ripping the magma to shreds and creating great clouds of gas and ash. If the magma is viscous but very low in dissolved gases, as in the case of dacites and rhyolites, it will ooze out slowly, like toothpaste being squeezed from a tube. Sometimes these pasty lavas extrude into domes or spines, such as that of Mount Pelée in Martinique (although this eruption started out very violently). A volcano can have different types of eruptions and the explosivity can vary even during one eruption. Gases tend to migrate towards the top of the magma chamber, so many eruptions start out explosively and become progressively more effusive as the gas is depleted.

Types of magma

A magma's gas content is critical to how explosive an eruption will be but so is its composition, because that largely determines its viscosity. Location is also really important, as the tectonic setting largely controls the composition of the magma. The *rheology* of a magma (the way in which it flows) depends on a number of factors, including chemical composition, temperature, the amount of dissolved gases and the proportion of solid materials such as crystals.

The classification of volcanic rocks (see Figure 2) is based on their silica (SiO_2) content and alkali (sodium (Na) and potassium (K)) content. Figure 2 includes rare minor varieties that are of great interest to geochemists but the main magma types are basalts, andesites, dacites and rhyolites.

The key factor in a magma's chemical composition is the amount of silica in the magma, which is found as silicon dioxide (SiO_2). The magmas that contain the least amount of silicon dioxide are the least viscous; these are the basaltic magmas (also called basic or mafic magmas). Basaltic magmas originate in the mantle's upper regions and erupt in a relatively pristine state, often referred to as 'primitive'. Basalt cools very rapidly, giving the minerals little chance to grow; the result is a fairly uniform,

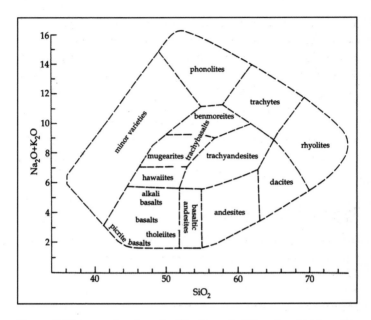

Figure 2 Diagram showing classification of different volcanic rocks. Silica content (SiO$_2$) is plotted against alkali content. (Modified from Francis, 1993.)

dark rock in which it is difficult to see the minerals with the naked eye. Basalts are usually dark in colour, because they are relatively rich in iron and magnesium. The main component minerals are feldspar and pyroxene, with smaller amounts of olivine. Some basalts are very rich in olivine, giving them a greenish hue. A famous example of a product of such an eruption is Green Sand Beach on the island of Hawaii.

Other types of magma – basaltic andesites, andesites, dacites and rhyolites – contain progressively higher amounts of silicon dioxide. These magmas, called silicic, acidic or evolved magmas, are usually lighter in colour than basalts and contain minerals such as feldspar and quartz. Evolved magmas come up from subduction zones, where a lot of mixing of old crust and new magma occurs. They are not pristine, unlike basalts, and are sometimes referred to as 'recycled' magmas.

The silicon dioxide content affects the viscosity of the magma because silicon and oxygen atoms form strong bonds in inter-linked tetrahedral groups – this is called *polymerisation*. The higher the percentage of silicon dioxide in the magma, the more polymerised (and therefore more viscous) it can be. Other fac-tors, such as the presence of other minerals or gases, can encour-age polymerisation (making the magma more viscous) or can break down the bonds between the silicon and oxygen (making magma more fluid). Water in the magma drastically decreases vis-cosity; carbon dioxide increases it. The amount of solid crystals also has a significant effect: the more solid crystals in the magma, the more viscous it will be. Basaltic magmas are typically only a few per cent crystals; in contrast, dacites can be as much as forty per cent crystals. Think of the crystals as like the dried fruit in a cake mix; any home-baker knows that a heavy fruit cake mix flows less easily than one with only a few scattered raisins.

Temperature also influences viscosity: the hotter the magma, the more easily it will flow. The temperature of magma varies with its composition (see Table 1) – basalts erupt at higher tem-peratures than andesites and other more silicic magmas. The melting temperature is commonly called the *liquidus* tempera-ture. Lava cools very quickly once it erupts, so if a remote sensing instrument detects erupting lava at a temperature of 1,000°C,

Table 1: Magma composition and temperature

Magma composition	Liquidus temperature (°C)
Basalt	1000–1250
Andesite	950–1200
Dacite	800–1100
Rhyolite	700–900

it could be either a particularly hot rhyolite or a basalt that has cooled to the point of being mostly solid. This causes some interesting problems when using remote sensing instruments to measure the temperature of lava and so deduce its composition: all we can say is that lavas can't be a particular composition because they are too hot. For example, a measured temperature of 1,200°C effectively rules out rhyolite and dacite but lava at 700°C could be anything. Since fluidity increases with temperature, the hotter basalts (at around 1,250°C) tend to flow more easily than the cooler ones. However, two types of magma at the same temperature (for example, basalt and andesite at 1,000°C) will not have the same viscosity: the more silicic magma (the andesite) will always be the more viscous.

The gas content of the different types of magma can also vary. Basalts have relatively low gas content, typically less than one per cent, and more silicic magmas generally have greater gas content; rhyolites can contain as much as five per cent. Generally, the more gas in the magma, the bigger the explosion, so the more silicic magmas are likely to be the more explosive.

To summarise, a volcano's explosivity is linked to the composition of its magma, which largely depends on the volcano's tectonic setting: mid-oceanic ridge volcanoes erupt basaltic magma, while subduction zones erupt more silicic magmas. The volcanoes around the Pacific Ring of Fire tend to have more explosive eruptions than those in Iceland and other places along the Mid-Atlantic Ridge and the Hawaiian volcanoes which erupt over a hot spot. There are exceptions to this general rule: some volcanoes in Iceland, such as Hekla and Eyjafjallajökull, have erupted explosively, while volcanoes in subduction zones, such as Masaya in Nicaragua, have been placid. Other factors come into play, such as the specific composition of the magma in a particular volcano, the interaction of magma with an overlying ice cap, the amount of gas in the magma and the plumbing system of the volcano.

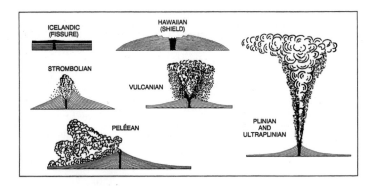

Figure 3 Major types of volcanic eruption showing their relative explosivity. (Modified from Simkin and Siebert, 1994.)

Types of eruptions

Volcanoes erupt in a variety of ways: some are very gentle, others make a big bang. There is no clear-cut way to classify the different types of volcanic eruptions but volcanologists tend to sort eruptions by their character or general behaviour; the biggest distinguishing factor is how explosive they are.

The classification of different types of volcanic eruptions was begun by the Italian scientist Giuseppe Mercalli, best known for his scale of earthquake intensity, which runs from *I* (detected only by instruments) to *XII* (intense – total destruction). Mercalli started the tradition of naming different types of volcanic eruptions after the places where they are most common; in order of the least explosive to the most they run from Hawaiian to Strombolian, Vulcanian, Peléean, Plinian and Ultraplinian. The last two are not named after a location; they honour Pliny the Younger, the Roman writer who gave us the first scientific written description of a volcanic eruption, that of Vesuvius in 79 CE. Some volcanologists like to add Icelandic eruptions to the mix, although others consider them to be a subset of Hawaiian eruptions.

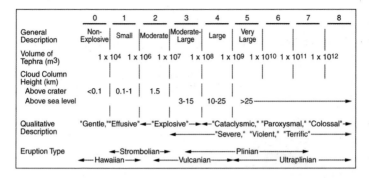

Figure 4 Diagram showing the criteria for the Volcano Explosivity Index (VEI). (Modified from Simkin and Siebert, 1994.)

Others add hydromagmatic (or phreatomagmatic) eruptions – caused by interaction of hot magma and water – as a separate character. Eruptions known as phreatic are those in which no new magma is erupted and the explosions are caused by still-hot magma that came from a previous eruption or that is still in the conduit.

More recently, volcanologists have developed a relative measure for classifying the size of eruptions, the Volcanic Explosivity Index (VEI), which runs from 0 to 8. The VEI of an eruption is not a precise number; it is derived from observers' descriptions as well as information about the volume and type of material erupted and the height of the eruption column above the volcano. No instrument can measure how big a volcanic eruption is; any classification is likely to be partly subjective.

Volcano shapes

The shape of a volcano can also give clues about its magma composition and predominant type of eruption. Planetary geologists

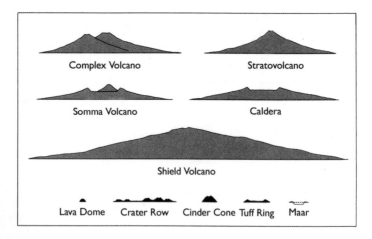

Figure 5 Major types of volcanoes. These schematic profiles are exaggerated vertically by a factor of two (for volcanoes shaded in gray) and a factor of four (for those shaded in black). Relative sizes are approximate. (Modified from Simkin and Siebert, 1994.)

often use the shape of volcanoes to infer eruption types and possible composition of the magma on other planets, where – for obvious reasons – lava samples are not available. Volcanoes do not always produce mountains or cones: effusive eruptions, such as *Hawaiian* and *Icelandic* types, produce long lava flows that often come out of many fissures rather than a single vent or source. If the lava flow is thin, copious and spreads out over long distances, it will form a lava plain. If lava flows from Hawaiian or Icelandic-type eruptions keep piling up on top of one another, they will eventually produce a 'shield volcano' (named for their shape, like a warrior's shield) such as Mauna Loa on Hawaii. Shield volcanoes frequently have large craters (*calderas*) in their centre, formed after large quantities of magma erupt from the magma chamber, leaving the chamber's roof without support and causing it to collapse. The largest volcanoes in the world are shield volcanoes.

In rare cases, the magma is viscous but contains little gas, so the lava is extruded rather than exploded and forms a *lava dome*. Lava domes are relatively small compared to other types of volcano, rarely exceeding a hundred metres in height. Their flanks are much steeper, usually sloping at 25 to 30°, than those of shield volcanoes, which typically have slopes of 4 to 8°. Domes are generally *monogenetic* (formed by a single eruption): once the eruption is over, the volcano will not erupt again. Unsurprisingly, monogenetic volcanoes are smaller than *polygenetic* volcanoes, such as shield volcanoes, which are formed by repeated eruptions over long periods.

Mildly explosive eruptions, such as Strombolian, form a small, steep-sided *cinder cone* around the vent, constructed from the fragments of lava (called bombs, cinder or, more rigorously, pyroclastics) that land around the vent. Strombolian cones are often monogenetic, though eruptions can last for many years (or, in the case of Stromboli, millennia). Because the falling fragments of lava tend to accumulate around the vent, most cones have steep and fairly uniform slopes. Some cones can be quite large: Stromboli is 924 metres high. Sunset Crater in Arizona and Parícutin in Mexico are other examples of Strombolian volcanoes. Cinder cones are the most widespread type of land volcano on Earth.

ENCELADUS

According to the Roman poet Virgil, the goddess Athena buried the giant Enceladus beneath Etna as punishment for his rebellion against the Olympian gods. Earthquakes were caused by the giant tossing and turning and eruptions were attributed to his fiery breath. His brother Mimas was thought to be buried beneath Vesuvius.

More explosive eruptions, such as Vulcanian, Peléean and Plinian, produce large quantities of pyroclastics. They produce cones, similar to Strombolian types but can also have lava flows, giving rise to classically shaped volcanoes, such as Mount Fuji in Japan. Such volcanoes, formed by the combination of layers of lava and pyroclastics, are called *stratovolcanoes* or *composite volcanoes*. Although stratovolcanoes look majestic and large, they are generally much smaller in volume than shield volcanoes. The beautiful, upswept shape of Mount Fuji and many other stratovolcanoes is caused by the evolution of volcanic activity as the volcano grows older. When these volcanoes are young, their eruptions tend to come from a single central conduit; as they age, fractures can open on the lower flanks, from which lava flows emerge. Explosive eruptions still happen at the summit and, gradually, the summit cone becomes steeper relative to the lower slopes. Erosion also modifies the volcano's profile: ash is more easily eroded than lava and erosion removes material from the upper slopes and deposits it around the base, flattening the lower slopes. Not all stratovolcanoes have Fuji's symmetry: when a volcano has a very large Plinian or Ultraplinian eruption, the top of the volcano can collapse into a caldera, 'cutting off' the top of the volcano. Another variation is the Somma type, named after the Vesuvius-Somma complex, which has calderas formed by very large eruptions, within which a new cone grows.

The number and shape of vents has a significant influence on the shape of a volcano. A volcano with more than one major vent can grow into a complex volcano and sometimes two vents erupt independently, resulting in two volcanoes growing together. Vents can be either like pipes, originating from deep inside the volcano and connected directly to the surface, or like fissures or cracks cutting down the flanks. A system of fissures or small vents that cut across the volcano in a well-defined direction is called a *rift zone*. Hekla in Iceland and Mauna Loa in Hawaii are rift zone volcanoes: their eruptions usually come from the long fissures, resulting in an elongated profile – although Mauna Loa is a shield volcano, its shape is more like an overturned canoe.

Some volcanoes, such as Mount Etna, have numerous pipe vents on their flanks, resulting in multiple cones dotting the landscape. New vents can open up fairly low on the volcano's flanks and eruptions can appear from almost anywhere, threatening anything that lies below.

Lava flows, pyroclastic flows and other volcanic products

Lava flows are most commonly the product of Hawaiian–type eruptions but can also occur during other eruptions, usually in their less violent phases. There are three main types of lava flows: *pahoehoe*, *aa* (or *a'a*) and *block* lavas. Hawaiian eruptions produce pahoehoe and aa flows: pahoehoe is smoother and easier to walk on than the rubbly, spiky aa. Both words come from Hawaiian: pahoehoe can be translated as 'easy to walk on', while aa literally means 'Ahhh! Ahhhh!' Anyone trekking over miles of pahoehoe might think the Hawaiians didn't know the meaning of 'easy' but they were comparing it to aa, which has lots of loose, spiny fragments on its surface. I cannot even imagine walking on it barefoot.

Pahoehoe lavas are the least viscous of the main types of lava flows and form ropes and coils as they cool on the surface. Ropy pahoehoe is most common when the flow is hot and runny. Pahoehoe lavas tend to creep slowly, though sometimes they form channels where the lava can run quickly: it's often possible to stand at the side of a pahoehoe flow and watch the moving lava quite safely. Glowing lobes (popularly known as 'toes'), ten to thirty centimetres long, advance, chill and stop within a metre or so. Pressure from within the lava flow keeps the flow moving, sprouting new toes so that a pahoehoe flow rapidly becomes a maze of individual lobes. A hike over a pahoehoe lava field would reveal other structures including *squeeze-ups*, places where the lava's surface fractures, allowing hot lava to squeeze up from beneath, and *tumuli*, formed by lava swelling up in a dome (or tumulus)-like way and breaking through the surface in a pattern of radial fractures, creating the broken mounds so common on the surface of Hawaiian pahoehoe flows. *Shelly lava* is another variation: these lavas have a very thin crust that can easily be broken by the pressure of a foot. Unfortunately, the void underneath the crust can be up to several metres deep, making shelly lava particularly hazardous if the flow underneath happens to be active! However, very recent pahoehoe lava flows can have a 'crunchy' crust, which has no empty space beneath.

Lava tubes or tunnels can form either in either aa or pahoehoe lavas, though the latter is rather more common. Tubes form when the upper side of lava flowing in a channel cools and solidifies, insulating the hot lava beneath, which remains liquid and flowing. When the lava supply is cut off, because the eruption ends or the flowing lava is diverted, the lava in the tube drains out, leaving it empty. If the roof subsequently collapses, the tube becomes visible from the surface (the collapsed parts are called *skylights*). Lava tubes, for example the Thurston Lava Tube on Hawaii Island, can become tourist attractions – exploring tubes is the volcanological equivalent of caving. The ceiling of the Thurston Tube is over six metres high in places but many tubes are much smaller.

Pahoehoe lava can turn into aa if, for example, it goes over a cliff and breaks up, but the reverse does not happen. Pahoehoe and aa lavas can form from the same magma; the effusion rate (the volume of a lava discharged in a certain time) is a major factor in determining which type of lava is produced. Higher effusion rates favour the formation of aa, which can be thought of as becoming more 'churned'. Aa lava is the most common type of lava flow on land. Aa flows are typically a few metres thick and have two distinct zones: an upper, rubbly part with a much larger part of solid lava beneath. The inner part of an aa flow cools slowly, insulated by the outer rubbly part. The lowest part of an aa flow also contains some rubble; as aa moves, the top spills over the front and is crushed by the advancing lava. Where aa lava is cut through, for example at a road cut, the dense interior part of the flow can be seen.

RECORD-BREAKING LAVA TUBES

The longest and deepest lava tube in the world is Kazumura Cave on the slopes of Kilauea. It is over sixty kilometres long, up to eighteen metres high and over one kilometre below ground level. The Undara lava tubes in Australia, where the lava has flowed some 160 kilometres from its source, are part of the longest lava flow from a single crater on Earth, formed in an eruption which happened about 190,000 years ago.

Block lavas are found on more silicic volcanoes. Some basaltic andesites or andesites form aa flows (never pahoehoe) but block lavas are a very typical product of andesite magmas. Their lava tends to flow rather sluggishly, in thick flows, often with flow fronts many metres high and with a surface covered in large blocks of lava, up to several metres across. They can present formidable obstacles to the explorer, as climbing over piles of angular blocks balancing precariously on top of each other is not easy. When the flanks of the volcano are steep, such as Arenal in Costa Rica, the fronts of blocky lavas can become detached from the main flow and tumble down. If these detached blocks are later run over by the lava flow, they can fuse together and become *autobrecciated*. Lava tubes are rare in andesitic lavas.

Very viscous lavas, such as dacites, may form *lava domes*, rather than lava flows, as the lava oozes upwards and spreads slowly on the surface. Some dacite lavas can form very thick, pasty flows, called *coulees*, somewhere between a lava flow and a lava dome in structure. Coulees are formed when the pasty lava flows over a slope steep enough to allow the mass to flow downhill for at least a short distance. The classic coulee is the Chao dacite in Chile, which consists of flow lobes about 300 metres high and pressure ridges (*ogives*) that resemble the ropy texture of pahoehoe but are much larger. The ridges can be many metres high and tens of metres apart. The flow's texture, particularly when viewed from a satellite, is quite distinct and for obvious reasons has been dubbed 'elephant skin'.

Rhyolites rarely form lava flows, as most eruptions of this magma are explosive, but there are a few examples, such as those around the Valles Caldera in New Mexico, USA. Rhyolites form domes and thick flows similar to dacites; however, they also have a unique and rather interesting type of flow: obsidian flows. Obsidian – volcanic glass – is black and glassy and breaks into sharp, pointed fragments. In dacite flows, the black, glassy obsidian is banded with a white, pumice-like material, making them very striking to look at. In these flows, the buoyant pumice rises through the denser layers of overlying obsidian, forming *diapirs*, a type of intrusion in which a more mobile material is forced into brittle overlying rocks.

Silicic lavas such as andesites, dacites and rhyolites often emerge in explosive eruptions rather than lava flows and the products of such eruptions tend to be much more destructive, ranging in size from *ash*, a fine powder that can cloak vast areas, to larger chunks, *bombs*, which can be a metre or more in diameter and tend to cause most damage near the vent. However, the most destructive and dangerous product of an explosive eruption is a *pyroclastic flow*: a fast-moving current of hot gases and rock fragments. (Pyroclastic comes from the Greek, meaning 'fire-broken'.) These flows – there are several types – do not occur in all eruptions but, when they do, they are devastating. Pyroclastic flows destroyed Pompeii and Herculaneum and, more recently, in 1902, the lovely city of St Pierre in Martinique. The damage done by lava flows pales in comparison with what pyroclastic flows can do.

Pyroclastic flows occur as a result of the collapse of an explosive eruption column. If the column of material erupting from the volcano is less dense than the surrounding air, it will rise convectively through the atmosphere. If it is denser than the surrounding air, once the momentum supplied by the eruption gas diminishes, the column collapses under the force of gravity and the mass of ash, pumice and hot gases falls and spreads around the volcano, moving as a fluid flow. Pyroclastic flows can move at speeds of a hundred kilometres per hour or more, faster than most cars and certainly faster than people trying to flee on foot; their energy can be so high that they flow uphill. A single pyroclastic flow may reach a hundred kilometres from its source and deposit a layer of ash, rock fragments and pumice several metres thick over countryside, villages and cities.

Pyroclastic flows that primarily contain pumice are sometimes called *pumice flows* and their deposits *ignimbrites*. Flows containing denser lava fragments are usually called *nuées ardentes* (French for 'glowing clouds'); the deposits they form are frequently called *block* and *ash* flows. The differences between pyroclastic flows or surges and *nuées ardentes* are subtle: technically, a *nuée ardente* is a flow of poorly-vesiculated magma (that is, magma that has very few gas bubbles). A *pyroclastic surge* is formed by the same process but has a lower overall density (that is, more gas) than a flow. They move very quickly and can even flow over water. They are sometimes called base surges, because of their similarity to the currents observed spreading along the ground after nuclear explosions. Pyroclastic surges often precede a denser pyroclastic flow. In general, the type of flow associated with a Peléean eruption is referred to as a *nuée ardente*, while those associated with Plinian eruptions are typically referred to as pyroclastic flows.

Hydromagmatic eruptions – a special type of eruption involving the interaction of water and magma – can lead to *mudflows*. Mudflows, also called *lahars*, can be extremely destructive. They are very hard to predict; they can be triggered by very small eruptions or even without any eruption. They occur on a wide variety of volcanoes but are most likely to form on steep-sided volcanoes, particularly those that are snow-capped. The one requirement is that the volcano needs to have large quantities of pyroclastics on its flanks, so mudflows are associated with stratocones.

Climatic effects of eruptions

Although the climatic changes produced by volcanic eruptions are usually small (rarely more than 1°C of global cooling), they can cause very noticeable effects. The eruption of Tambora in Indonesia in 1815, the last recorded Ultraplinian eruption, caused 1816 to be known in New England and Europe as 'the year without a summer' – temperatures in Europe were about 10°C cooler than normal for that time of year. Fortunately, Ultraplinian eruptions are very rare. Taupo in New Zealand had a cataclysmic Ultraplinian eruption in 186 CE, which undoubtedly affected the world's climate.

Large, highly explosive eruptions of the Plinian and Ultraplinian types inject large amounts of sulphur-containing gases into the stratosphere, where the sulphur combines with water vapour to form fine clouds of tiny sulphuric acid droplets that can remain in the stratosphere for several years. These 'aerosol' (suspensions of fine solid particles or liquid droplets in a gas) clouds appear to be the main contributor to global cooling, as the droplets both absorb solar radiation and scatter it back to space, resulting in a slight decrease in average temperatures around the world.

However, the effects can be more complicated; volcanic eruptions also affect ozone levels through the production of hydrochloric acid, which destroys ozone. Fortunately, most volcanic hydrochloric acid is confined to the troposphere and is washed out by rain, but studies after the 1991 eruptions of Pinatubo in the Philippines and Mount Hudson in Chile showed a fifteen to twenty per cent loss of ozone at high latitudes and more than fifty per cent loss over Antarctica. Since the hydrochloric acid from eruptions does not reach the stratosphere, and therefore doesn't have the opportunity to interact with ozone, another mechanism must be operating. It appears that aerosols generated by the eruptions provide surfaces upon which chemical reactions take place; the aerosols interact with chlorine- and bromine-bearing compounds from human-made CFCs (chloro-fluorocarbon gases), aggravating their effect. This is a temporary effect, as volcanic aerosols settle out of the stratosphere after two to three years. Although volcanic eruptions produce carbon dioxide gas, which can add to the atmosphere's burden of green-house gases and so contribute to global warming, this effect is very minor when compared to the amount of carbon dioxide contributed by human activities.

GHOSTS AND MONSTERS

An interesting consequence of the Tambora eruption was that the weather was so bad that it trapped three friends indoors during a holiday in Switzerland. One of them, Lord Byron, suggested a contest: who could write the scariest horror story? The winner was Mary Shelley, who penned one of the most famous of all time, *Frankenstein*. Lord Byron made his own immortal contribution during that year, with his poem 'Darkness'.

By far the most significant climatic effect of volcanic eruptions is the temporary lowering of global temperatures. Large eruptions in recent times (such as that of Pinatubo in 1991) have reduced global warming. Before the eruptions of El Chichón in Mexico in 1982, it was generally thought that suspended ash particles in the upper atmosphere blocked out sunlight, thus lowering temperatures. However, when scientists compared the climatic effects of the El Chichón eruption to that of the 1980 eruption of Mount St Helens in Washington State, they found that although St Helens had injected a larger amount of ash into the atmosphere, its eruption lowered global temperatures by only 0.1°C, while El Chichón caused a change of nearly 0.5°C because it emitted a much greater quantity of sulphur-rich gases; about forty times more by some estimates.

3

Hawaiian and Icelandic eruptions: fire fountains and lava lakes

Hawaiian and Icelandic eruptions are the most gentle and benign of all. These types of eruptions occur mainly on islands over the Mid-Atlantic Ridge (such as Iceland) or over a hot spot (such as Hawaii) but they can occur elsewhere, such as in the East African Rift Valley. The magma erupted is high-temperature, low-viscosity basalt, with a low gas content. The eruption is dominantly effusive, with a VEI of only 0 or 1. The most common products of this type of eruption are pahoehoe and aa lava flows, often erupting from long fissures rather than a single vent or source. The flows can be tens of kilometres long and spread over vast areas but are quite thin, sometimes less than a metre high. In Hawaiian eruptions, lava also spurts out as fire fountains, one of the most beautiful of Nature's spectacles. When the main product of an eruption is a fissure-fed lava flow that spreads out but forms no edifice, the eruption is sometimes called Icelandic.

In the Earth's ancient history, *flood basalts*, which can be thought of as particularly large Icelandic or Hawaiian eruptions, erupted huge volumes of lava and formed vast lava plains. The volume of lava on the Columbia River Basalts (or Plateau) in the western US, which flowed between seventeen and fifteen million years ago, is a staggering 170,000 cubic kilometres, with individual flows up to twenty to thirty metres thick, extending for hundreds of kilometres. Other well-known examples are the Deccan Traps in India and the Siberian Traps in Russia. 'Traps' comes from an old Swedish word for staircase; the topography of flood basalts is usually step-like, because the broken-up upper parts of the flows erode more quickly than the solid lower parts, creating a step pattern over the lava field. In terms of lava volume and the amount of volcanic gases they put into the atmosphere, flood basalts were truly catastrophic eruptions. Fortunately, flood basalts are now mostly found on other planets; they may be occurring on Jupiter's moon Io and they have definitely happened on other planets in the distant past. The maria on the Moon are also flood basalts.

The single modern example of an eruption that can be considered a flood basalt is that of Laki, in Iceland, in 1783, which poured out the largest lava flow in historic times. The eruption was a major environmental disaster for Iceland: huge quantities of sulphur dioxide were spewed out and about a hundred million tonnes of sulphuric acid formed as atmospheric aerosols. Although the eruption did not kill anyone directly, its consequences were disastrous for farmland, animals and humans alike: clouds of hydrofluoric acid and sulphur dioxide compounds caused the deaths of over half of Iceland's livestock and, ultimately, the deaths – mostly from starvation – of about 9,000 people, a third of the population. The climatic effects of the eruption were felt elsewhere in Europe; the winter of 1783–4 was noted as being particularly cold. Benjamin Franklin, the American Ambassador to France, was the first to discuss in print the connection between the Laki eruption, the 'blue haze' seen across many parts of Europe and the harsh winter.

The Laki flows were not only very large in volume (nearly fifteen cubic kilometres) but were discharged at very high rates. In general, the higher the discharge (or effusion) rate, the further a flow can travel before it cools. During the first forty-eight days of the eruption, four to five flows were produced, with an average discharge rate of 2,200 cubic metres per second. The lava advanced rapidly; up to seventeen kilometres in one day. In all, the eruption lasted eight months and covered an area of 565 square kilometres. The lava poured out of a fissure system twenty-seven kilometres long, with over one hundred craters. Unique in historic times (and given the catastrophe that it caused, let's hope it will remain so), Laki is not only of great interest to terrestrial volcanologists but also to planetary volcanologists; the very large, rapidly moving flows enable them to be considered as analogies for flows on the Moon, Mars and Venus. Several studies of the congealed flows on these bodies suggest that they were erupted at very high discharge rates.

While mild compared with other types of eruptions, Icelandic and Hawaiian eruptions are awe-inspiring and extremely photogenic. The typical vent of an Icelandic or Hawaiian eruption is a fissure; as the fissure opens at the start of the eruption and magma comes to the surface, *fire fountains* form. As the lucky few who have been able to see them shooting red lava and hot gases into the sky can attest, fire fountains are truly dramatic and when several fire fountains are aligned along a fissure, they create a breathtaking *curtain of fire*. Fire fountains are not the result of explosions but of the rapid expansion of gas in the magma. Gases migrate to the top of the magma chamber and concentrate there; when this gas-rich magma erupts at the start of the eruption, fire fountains occur, as the rapidly expanding gases fragment the fluid magma and the mixture of gas and fragments shoots out into the air. Fire fountains can last hours or days, frequently fluctuating in intensity. The fragments of lava thrown out accumulate near the fissure, forming spatter cones or spatter ramparts. (*Spatter* is a generic term for large fragments ejected by either fire fountains or Strombolian eruptions.) These hot, fluid fragments become flattened during impact.

Fire fountains are perhaps the most spectacular volcanological phenomenon but bubbling *lava lakes* come close. Lava lakes come about when magma stands high in the volcanic conduit (the pipe leading from the magma chamber to the vent) but not high enough to spill over the crater. Lava lakes occur during Hawaiian or Strombolian eruptions and some remain active for years or even decades. Lava lakes are rare on Earth (although they are common on Io) and, because they are often deep inside craters, are not easy to see. The most recent lava lakes on Earth can be found in the Erta Ale volcano in the Danakil Depression, Ethiopia, Mount Erebus in Antarctica, Nyaragongo in Zaire and Kilauea in Hawaii. The Halemaumau pit in the Kilauea caldera housed a lava lake that was active almost continuously from 1823 to 1924. It was a well-known tourist attraction: Volcano House, which was built to house its visitors, is still a working hotel.

I've been lucky enough to view two lava lakes. The first, on Mount Etna, associated with a summit Strombolian eruption, was deep within the mountain's summit crater: I had to lean precariously over the edge and wait until the steam and gas plume cleared before I could catch a glimpse of it. In contrast, the Kupaianaha lava pond, created during the Pu'u O'o eruption on Kilauea, was a major tourist attraction; I was just one of many who trekked over miles of lava to see it. The Kupaianaha lava pond was not a classic lava lake, hence its different designation, as it was not fed directly from the volcano's conduit but rather by a subsidiary vent on the volcano's north-east rift. Sadly, it is no longer active. At the time of writing, Erta Ale contained an active lava lake and so did Mount Erebus – both places that are hard to get to. Perhaps Kilauea or Mauna Loa will provide us with another lake in the near future.

The Krafla eruption, Iceland, 1975–83

The Krafla region has been volcanically active for some 200,000 years. Today, this completely alien landscape is characterised by vast expanses of black lava – if you ever wanted to walk on the Moon, this may be the next best thing. Krafla volcano itself is only 800 metres high and has not erupted for over 10,000 years. Volcanologists' interest in Krafla centres on the region's major fissure swarm, which is about a hundred kilometres long and up to ten kilometres wide, trending north-south. The fissure region has seen many eruptions but they do not happen frequently; the last eruption before 1975 was in 1724, an eruption known as the Mývatn Fires, after the nearby Lake Mývatn. The 1975–83 eruption became known as the *Krafla Fires*. The Krafla Fires were a series of eruptions rather than a single event. The activity was truly awe-inspiring: rows of fire fountains up to fifty metres high erupted from fissures and large quantities of basaltic lavas poured out. Best of all, there was little danger to observers; the eruption was truly a photographer's delight. The volcano was wonderfully co-operative in its eruption pattern, with inflation and deflation (the ground moving up and down) signalling outpourings of lava.

The inflation-deflation pattern is the most interesting aspect of the Krafla Fires. Immediately after an eruption, the caldera floor and fissure swarm subsided, sinking up to two metres and widening as much as 1.5 metres. For weeks or months before a new eruption, the ground slowly rose (seven to ten millimetres a day at the centre of the caldera floor) as the underlying magma chamber expanded with the influx of new magma from below. When inflation reached a critical level and pressure in the chamber exceeded the strength of surrounding rock, seismic activity increased. This was followed by rapid deflation, which indicated that magma had migrated sideways from the chamber into the fissure zone north and south of the main Krafla caldera. From 1975 to 1979, most of the magma migrated sideways and resulted in small surface eruptions. The eruptions between 1979 and 1984 were larger, as more magma poured out of the surface fissures.

The inflation-deflation pattern is a manifestation of what was, and is still, happening below Iceland's surface; Krafla gives us a view of the deeper levels within the Earth. Krafla is a surface expression of the rifting of two tectonic plates along the Mid-Atlantic Ridge and its pattern of activity gives us clues as to the workings of plate rifting.

Eruptions are not often recorded at Krafla but, when they are, they come in clusters. During the volcano's centuries-long quiet intervals, plate movements build up stress, which is eventually released by short bursts of rifting and volcanic activity. This means that plates are not moving apart smoothly but abruptly, in fits and starts.

Kilauea and the Pu'u O'o eruption, Hawaii, 1983–present

This long-lived eruption – the longest and most voluminous rift eruption in recorded history – has been viewed by countless visitors to the island of Hawaii. It has changed Hawaii, adding land (more than a square kilometre at the time of writing) but destroying several communities and the once-famous Black Sand Beach. For volcanologists, photographers and volcano enthusiasts the eruption has been fantastic: the relatively easy access and amount and quality of instrumentation have enabled scientists to study this eruption in greater depth than any other. Hawaiian eruptions are understood significantly better than they were before 1983; even locals talk about the island 'before the eruption', as if it were the only one that really matters.

The magma chamber on Kilauea lies at a shallow depth, so that the influx of new magma makes the volcano inflate in a way that is easily measured by tiltmeters and other instruments. This inflation is also associated with seismic activity, making eruptions on Kilauea relatively easy to predict in terms of when and where they are likely to start. This eruption began like many on Kilauea: the prediction was that it would start from Kilauea's East Rift Zone; some scientists even camped out nearby so as not to miss the event. On the morning of 3 January 1983, the ground cracked open and a line of fire fountains spurted out from the fissure, delighting those lucky enough to be there. The eruption seemed to stop after three weeks but that turned out to be merely a lull in a series of eruptive episodes. Over the years, lava flowed in tubes down to the ocean, creating plumes where it entered the water, a lava pond developed at Kupaianaha, the cone of Pu'u O'o grew bigger and, eventually, a new lava shield grew on the western flank of Pu'u O'o.

The main crater – a beautiful sight from a plane or helicopter – is still active. Tourists still flock to observe the plumes where the lava falls into the ocean and to hunt for breakouts of the lava on the surface. The island still expands and, although many have lost their homes to the lava, there have been very few deaths. Pele, goddess of volcanoes, continues to make herself a bigger home.

Fernandina, Galapagos Islands, 1968 and 1995

The Galapagos, known for their remarkable fauna, are volcanic islands, some of which are still active. Fernandina is about 1,476 metres high and has the largest caldera in the Galapagos. It last erupted in early 2005 but it erupts frequently, in spectacular Hawaiian-type eruptions. The volcano is a shield volcano, with a large summit caldera, which collapsed from about 600 metres deep to about 1,000 metres deep during the eruption of 1968, when it was estimated that about two cubic kilometres of magma was withdrawn, leaving the void that allowed it to collapse. Caldera collapses are very rare; this event was the largest caldera collapse on a basaltic volcano in recent history. The current dimensions of the caldera are approximately 6.6 kilometres by four kilometres by one kilometre deep. Following the collapse, the caldera became partially filled by a water lake. During the 1970s and 1980s, eruptions from fissures encircling the caldera caused lava flows to pour into the lake, making it boil. An eruption in 1988 caused the collapse of a section of the east caldera wall about a cubic kilometre in extent, producing a debris-avalanche deposit that covered much of the caldera floor and destroyed the lake.

MISSION: TORTOISE RESCUE

When the Cerro Azul volcano erupted on Isabela Island in 1998, the authorities decided to evacuate its threatened rare tortoises. Some were flown out by helicopter but some had to be carried over rough terrain by human rescuers. Since the tortoises weigh some 200 kilogrammes, this can't have been easy. Eruptions on the Galapagos may be innocuous to human life or property but they can be a local ecological disaster.

Fernandina differs from the Hawaiian shields like Mauna Loa and Kilauea in that it does not have prominent rift zones cutting along its flanks. The volcano's shape is somewhat different from a typical Hawaiian shield: Fernandina has steep slopes, up to 36°, on its upper flanks, which may be related to the ring fissures encircling the caldera, from which many lava flows have come, but the correlation between the fissures and the slopes is not clear. Some scientists have suggested that volcanoes such as Fernandina may be a better terrestrial analogy for Martian volcanoes such as Olympus Mons and Alba Patera than the Hawaiian volcanoes: several Martian volcanoes have large calderas encircled by a series of arcuate fissures. Fernandina has had flank eruptions, such as that of 1995, which lasted ten weeks. In this eruption, a radial fissure opened relatively low on the south-western flank, at about 250 metres. From here, lava flows spewed out that travelled some nine kilometres down to the ocean and covered an area of over eight square kilometres.

The island is not inhabited by humans but the eruption was tragic for Fernandina's wildlife. The island's marine iguanas use the Fernandina caldera as a nesting ground; every year they make the long journey across the island, up the volcano and down the caldera to lay their eggs by the lake. Unfortunately, the 1988 eruption interrupted the nesting season and destroyed the eggs on the caldera floor, which were nearly ready to hatch. The lake completely dried out after this eruption and has not been restored: the iguanas, however, keep coming, oblivious to the impending danger of a new eruption. The boiling coastal waters killed fish and caused fish that normally live at depth to rise to the surface. The fish feast attracted many birds, and soon birds as well as fish, iguanas and other animals were dying. Luckily, the lava flows stopped a mile short of the wildlife haven of Cape Hammond. On the positive side, the eruption built new land, extending the coastline by several hundred metres.

Erta Ale, Ethiopia, 1967–present

The Erta Ale volcano is a broad (fifty kilometres across) and relatively low (613 metres high) shield volcano with a pair of beautiful and regularly active lava lakes. Sometimes Erta Ale's crater has two active lakes, sometimes both crust over and are inactive. Erta Ale is one of the best places to study lava lakes on Earth; unfortunately, it is located at the bottom of the Danakil Depression, 155 metres below sea level, one of the hottest and most inhospitable locations on Earth, where summertime temperatures can reach more than 50°C. The lakes were discovered in 1967 but, due to their inaccessibility, ground monitoring has been sporadic. In the local language, 'Erta Ale' means 'fuming mountain' so it is a fair bet that the volcano has been active many times. The local Danakil tribes believe that devils live in the crater, which is not surprising; Erta Ale would be many people's idea of Hell, volcanologists excepted. For those who can get there, the night-time view is unforgettable: basaltic lava fills a lake about a hundred metres in diameter, with red cracks glowing across its surface; fire fountains spurt and the crater walls smoulder where the crust breaks against the rock.

Erta Ale is within the East African Rift Valley, a site of intercontinental volcanism. The valley extends from Ethiopia to Tanzania, with the Red Sea at its northern end. The volcanoes along the rift are extremely varied in their activity: Mount Kenya is no longer active, Kilimanjaro, the highest point in Africa, still vents steam and gases, and one of the world's most interesting active volcanoes, Ol Doinyo Lengai, is located in the Rift Valley. Further west, two volcanoes in Zaire, Nyamuragira and Nyiragongo, are frequently active and both have had lava lakes. Nyiragongo was the cause of many deaths in 1977, when its persistent lava lake suddenly drained through a series of cracks. In less than an hour, twenty-two million cubic metres of low-viscosity basaltic lava rushed down the volcano's sides at about sixty kilometres per hour. Some compared it to the bursting of a dam. About seventy people died in that tragic event and several hundred more were left homeless. Nyiragongo has since sent massive lava flows down its flanks but the lava lake-draining has, thankfully, not been seen again. Thanks to its inhospitable, isolated location, Erta Ale does not pose a significant hazard to human life.

Viewing Hawaiian eruptions

Hawaiian and Icelandic eruptions are the easiest and safest to view; all you need is an easily accessible location. The Pu'u O'o eruption of Kilauea has delighted visitors for many years and is currently the best option for volcano watchers. The hazards of travelling in Ethiopia make the lava lake at Erta Ale difficult to get to, although worth it for those who make it. Fernandina erupts on average about once a decade and is not particularly accessible as the Galapagos Islands are protected; during an eruption, visitors would probably only be able to watch from a boat some way offshore although this would still be an incredible sight. If Krafla erupts again it would be a treat, as volcanologists predict a spectacular show. The Icelandic government also makes access relatively easy, placing responsibility on visitors to look after their own safety. It is a wonderful country to visit, with little in the way of fences and few warning signs.

The dangers of Hawaiian and Icelandic eruptions are not hard to avoid. Close to a lava lake, the terrain can be unstable and may collapse, so visitors should walk around at a distance to make sure the chosen viewing place is solid and not an overhang. For the same reason, do not get too close to where lava enters the ocean. Lava creates new land but ocean waves erode it, often creating lava benches. People have been killed because they were in the wrong place at the wrong time when a bench collapsed. Lava entering water tends to vaporise instantly into steam, creating explosions. This can also happen when lava travels over wet areas, such as boggy or marshy ground. Iceland has fields of rootless cones (or *pseudocraters*) created by just this process. 'Rootless' means that no vent caused the cones to form; instead they were created by explosions as lava came into contact with waterlogged ground. Walking over shelly lava is dangerous, even if an eruption has stopped, as the draining lava can leave big voids. Falling into one of these voids could cause serious injury or even death; falling into an active lava tube would be almost certain death. Fire fountains are easy to view, as long as one stays out of range of the falling fragments. Lava flows are even safer: pahoehoe flows, in particular, tend to move slowly and it is possible to stand right next to them, watching the pahoehoe toes form and red lava ooze out.

4

Strombolian eruptions: Nature's fireworks

Stromboli, one of the volcanic Aeolian Islands which lie off the coast of Italy, has been known to be active almost continuously for over 2,500 years. Strombolian eruptions are characterised by mild to moderate explosions punctuated by quiet periods ranging from less than a minute to half an hour or more. The cyclic rhythm of Strombolian eruptions can last for centuries, making such volcanoes very reliable for eruption-watching. Stromboli itself, with its millennia-long activity, is the prime example, but Yasur in Vanuatu also qualifies. However, some Strombolian eruptions take place on monogenetic volcanoes, which have only one period of activity and then shut off for good.

Strombolian eruptions are, in general, fuelled by basaltic magma but it tends to be a more viscous type than that involved in Hawaiian and Icelandic-type eruptions. The gas content also tends to be higher. The gases coalesce into large bubbles, which, when they reach the surface, burst and throw out lava fragments. Therefore, instead of coming out easily and quietly from the magma, generating fire fountains and flows, gases come out more explosively in Strombolian activity. The VEI of most Strombolian eruptions is 1 or 2. Lava flows are typically shorter and thicker than those in Hawaiian and Icelandic eruptions. The explosions, usually accompanied by loud bangs, shoot lava high above the ground; the smaller fragments can reach tens of metres high.

The repeated explosions and falling lava bombs build steep cones around the main vent. Predominantly Strombolian volcanoes tend to be cones, quite steep but puny compared to Hawaiian volcanoes or stratocones. Stromboli itself is 924 metres high and only 12.2 square kilometres in area.

Strombolian eruptions are common on numerous basaltic volcanoes around the world. Stromboli and Yasur are special cases where the activity has been extremely long-lasting, but shorter periods of Strombolian activity have occurred in volcanoes as diverse as Arenal in Costa Rica, Fuji in Japan, La Palma in the Canary Islands, Pacaya and Fuego in Guatemala and Askja in Iceland.

Stromboli, Aeolian Islands, Italy

Stromboli has long been known as the 'Lighthouse of the Mediterranean'; the earliest records of eruptions go back to about 300 BCE. It erupts almost continuously; the relatively small explosions can be seen every twenty minutes or so, spraying glowing lava fragments and gas hundreds of metres above the vent and creating breathtaking fireworks. It is the prime destination for those who want to be sure to see volcanic activity, though it is not always safe to climb to the top. When safe, it can be climbed easily: there is a path; though steep, no special skills are needed. From the top, the explosions can be seen in their full glory.

The nearly continuous show is a result of the large, shallow magma chamber located beneath the volcano, probably fed continuously from a source in the mantle. Stromboli is a stratovolcano and has had more violent explosive eruptions in the past: old deposits indicate that Plinian eruptions have happened here. Even now, the volcano's activity is not always mild. In 1930, the volcano had a violent eruption that triggered earthquakes and even a tsunami. Several people were killed by pyroclastic flows and falling blocks. This could happen again, but most of the time,

Stromboli is a well-behaved, archetypal location for the activity that's been named after it.

One of Stromboli's major features is the *Sciara del Fuoco* (Trail of Fire), a horseshoe-shaped, deep, very steep scar on the volcano's north-western flank, probably formed by a huge collapse or landslide at least 5,000 years ago. The Sciara begins near the summit and travels all the way to sea level, by which time it is about 1,500 metres wide and is confined within 300-metre-high walls. The Sciara is a natural channel along which lava is carried down to the sea; its high walls keep the island's residents safe and allow people to live on the flanks of a very active volcano.

Yasur, Tanna Island, Vanuatu

Yasur, known as the 'Lighthouse of the Pacific', is located at the south-eastern tip of Tanna Island, one of the islands in the Vanuatu group. It is a bare, 361-metre-high cone with a nearly circular, 400-metre-wide summit crater. Historic records are limited: Captain Cook made the first report of its activity in 1774 but we know that Yasur was active before that. Like Stromboli, Yasur is a stratovolcano that has had more violent eruptions in the past but the majority these days are Strombolian or, occasionally, mild Vulcanian. Yasur, and the other islands in the Vanuatu group, lie on a subduction zone, where the eastward-moving Indo–Australian Plate is being subducted beneath the westward-moving Pacific Plate. There are other active volcanoes in the Vanuatu group but Yasur is the most continuously active.

Yasur is very easy to visit; four-wheel drive vehicles can get close to the summit and visitors have only a short hike to the crater rim, from where they have a magnificent view of the erupting vents. At times, Yasur has had a lava lake within its crater, making it even more worth seeing. Usually, one or two vents are erupting and explosions occur several times per hour. Some explosions deposit bombs outside the rim of the crater, in the viewing area, so visitors must take particular care to watch out for larger explosions and keep an eye on the trajectory of the bombs.

An interesting but little-known fact about Yasur is that it is responsible for a significant contribution of sulphur dioxide to the atmosphere. Recent studies have shown that the sulphur dioxide emission from Yasur contributes some one to two per cent of estimated global volcanic emissions to the atmosphere and about 1.5 to 2.5 per cent to the troposphere.

Sunset Crater, Arizona, USA

Sunset Crater is a monogenetic volcano, built over a relatively short period of time between 1064 and 1250 (although the exact dates are not known) by a single eruption or series of eruptions. It is not expected to become active again. Parícutin in Mexico, the famous volcano that started erupting in a cornfield in 1943 and ended its activity in 1952, is another volcano of this type. Monogenetic volcanoes like these are formed by Strombolian eruptions that build a relatively small cone around the vent.

Sunset Crater is only 300 metres high. It is located in the San Francisco volcanic field, north of Flagstaff in Arizona, which has about 400 similar cones. The first eruption was probably quite small, perhaps starting similarly to Parícutin, as a small crack in the earth. Rapidly, the fissure extended to about fifteen kilometres, with fire fountains erupting all along its length. The activity became localised at the north-western end of the fissure, with Strombolian explosions sending lava fragments into the air. The larger fragments fell near the vent and started building the cone. The eruptions that created Sunset Crater also formed two lava flows, which flowed out before the end of the explosive phase. The second flow, Bonito, took away parts of the cone, carrying them like rafts on its surface.

Sunset Crater's activity, nearly a thousand years ago, had a great influence on the local indigenous people, the Sinagua. There is evidence that they initially fled unharmed but many came back later and thrived on soil made fertile by the volcanic ash that blanketed and fertilised the surrounding lands. The Sunset Crater eruption has been credited as the trigger for one of the USA's first population explosions.

Eldfell, Heimaey Island, Iceland

Eldfell is also a Strombolian monogenetic volcano. Located on the island of Heimaey, off the west coast of Iceland, Eldfell had one of the most interesting eruptions in history in terms of its impact on local people. The eruption, which began in 1973, was totally unexpected; no precursors had been noticed and no volcanic activity had occurred on the island for several thousand years. In the early hours of the morning of 23 January 1973, local residents were awakened by explosions from a 1,800-metre-long fissure that had opened on the flanks of their long-dormant volcano, Helgafell. Fire fountains more than 200 metres high burst forth, forming a continuous and stunning curtain of fire. The fissure was less than one kilometre from the island's town, almost literally in residents' gardens. Icelanders have long lived with volcanic eruptions and the townspeople were calm and organised. Within a few hours, the island was almost completely evacuated as the island's fishing fleet carried most of the residents to the mainland; by the end of the next day, all had found lodging in people's homes.

Within two days, the activity along the fissure had become concentrated and Strombolian in character, building a cone over 110 metres high. Given that most residents had been evacuated, the eruption did not threaten lives but it soon became clear that it could threaten the islanders' livelihood. In early February, a massive lava flow begun to advance towards the harbour, narrowing its entrance and threatening eventually to destroy it. Since the islanders lived by fishing, that would have meant total economic disaster. Realising that something must be done to save the harbour, residents, helped by volunteers from the mainland, began a bold and historic fight against the lava flow. First, they sprayed water on the flow front, which had the effect of making it cool and harden more quickly, forming a barrier. The effort escalated into a system of large water pumps in the harbour, with a network of pipes to carry the water to the flow front. Elsewhere, cooled lava was bulldozed to form a barrier. It was the first genuinely successful attempt to divert a lava flow and a truly heroic effort, with volunteers working in very difficult conditions. From its beginning, in February, to its end, in July, over one million cubic metres of seawater were pumped onto the lava flows, converting about six million cubic metres of molten lava into solid rock. Although many houses were destroyed by the eruption, the harbour was saved and the lava flows added about 2.5 square kilometres to the area of the island. Although there have been several attempts since to divert lava on other volcanoes, the Heimaey effort remains the most outstandingly successful and a testimony to the ingenuity and hard work of people who refused to let nature destroy their lives.

Viewing Strombolian eruptions

Strombolian eruptions are stunning and, like Hawaiian and Icelandic eruptions, rarely kill anyone. Volcanoes like Stromboli and Yasur are ideal for those who want to view and photograph eruptions, as they are constantly active. Other volcanoes where Strombolian activity frequently occurs include Mount Etna in Sicily and Mount Erebus in Antarctica (but a special permit is needed to visit Erebus). Volcanoes in Iceland also exhibit Strombolian activity, as do some in South America. Strombolian activity is actually more common around the world than Hawaiian or Icelandic.

The fact that they are popular with tourists does not mean they don't pose dangers! Hiring a local guide is highly recommended. The major danger of Strombolian eruptions is the bombs they hurl sometimes hundreds of metres above the vent. It is prudent to watch the activity from a long and very safe distance before coming in close. Violent explosions can occur unexpectedly, so the 'safe distance' can only be a guideline. If bombs come towards you, don't turn your back and run. Instead, watch their trajectories, and move aside if one is coming right at you. Strombolian activity usually has intervals of a few minutes to tens of minutes between explosions, so that time can be used to get further away to safety.

5

Vulcanian and Peléean eruptions: great explosions and deadly glowing clouds

The island that gave its name not only to the world's volcanoes but also to the Vulcanian type of eruption is another of the Aeolian archipelago. Vulcano, a small island neighbour of Stromboli, has been erupting, on and off, for millennia. The ancient Romans believed that Vulcan, the blacksmith god, lived inside Vulcano. Peléean eruptions are generally more explosive than Vulcanian and often accompanied by deadly pyroclastic flows. They are named after Mount Pelée in Martinique, whose 1902 eruption killed nearly 30,000 people.

Vulcanian eruptions are more explosive than Strombolian and their magma, generally made up of andesites, dacites and rhyolites, tends to be more silicic. Vulcanian explosions are larger than Strombolian, sometimes destroying part of the volcano; they often start out by blowing off the volcano's cap, throwing out fragments of older rocks, and clearing a clogged conduit. The bombs are larger and reach further and the lava flows that some-times form tend to be more viscous. In a typical Vulcanian erup-tion, large quantities of ash rise up in a black eruption column, which can reach twenty or more kilometres in height; the ash is frequently deposited over large areas. Vulcanian bombs often have angular edges, as the magma is too viscous for the bombs to round off during flight. The typical product of a Vulcanian eruption is a stratocone, usually larger than those formed by Strombolian activity. Examples of Vulcanian eruptions include Vulcano, La Soufrière on St Vincent, Merapi in Java, Manam in Papua New Guinea and Sakurajima in Japan.

Peléean eruptions have been responsible for much of the death and destruction caused by volcanoes, because of their main characteristic: pyroclastic flows. Often known as *nuées ardentes*, these deadly mixtures of hot gases, ash, pumice and lava fragments destroy everything in their path. The other major characteristic of Peléean eruptions is lava domes, formed by very viscous, slowly extruded lavas.

Like Vulcanian eruptions, this viscous magma is responsible for a big bang and the ejection of an eruption cloud. The build-up of magma inside the crater as a pasty dome is an indication that trouble lies ahead. The pressure builds and eventually the dome explodes. If the resulting blast is directed sideways, the eruption column is propelled downhill, under the force of gravity, as a deadly *nuée ardente*. The gases and fine particles rise above the main flow but its dense core speeds downhill (or sometimes even uphill) with enormous energy, flattening and killing everything in its path. The temperature inside these flows can be hot enough to melt glass, as evidenced by the molten glass found after the eruption of Mount Pelée.

Peléean eruptions usually occur in stratovolcanoes. They typically discharge deadly *nuées ardentes* but they can end quietly, with the formation of a lava dome or spine inside the main crater vent, formed as the very pasty lava is pushed up slowly; usually these spines eventually collapse. Peléean eruptions have happened in La Soufrière on St Vincent, Mayon in the Phillippines, Merapi in Java and Bezymianny in Russia.

Vulcano, Italy

This island volcano is about 500 metres high and just over twenty-one square kilometres in area. Its active crater, the Fossa, sits atop a cone inside the youngest caldera on the island. Vulcano was more or less uninhabited before 1870, when it was acquired by a wealthy Scottish businessman, James Stevenson. The Scotsman intended to mine the sulphur and alum in the island to supply his chemical works in Glasgow. His operation was short-lived; in 1888, the Fossa crater woke up in a violent explosion. Part of the eruption was witnessed by the Italian scientist Mercalli, pioneer of volcano classification, and so this eruption therefore became the primary example of the Vulcanian type. The initial explosion threw out old fragments of the volcano and was followed by many other eruptions of the same type. Large quantities of ash were produced, blanketing Vulcano. Incandescent bombs, up to a metre in diameter, were ejected, some landing ten kilometres from the vent. The ejection of large numbers of *breadcrust* bombs was a characteristic of this eruption. Breadcrust bombs are rounded or angular bombs with a smooth glassy crust broken by cracks. They are formed when fragments of viscous, gas-rich magma are ejected from the vent. The outer crust cools quickly but the interior remains hot and continues to froth as gases are released. The expansion of the interior causes the crust to crack, like a loaf of bread in an oven.

The eruption did not cause any fatalities but it devastated the island. The huge explosions were heard on the neighbouring island of Lipari and even broke windows there. Vulcano has not had any major eruptions since 1888 but it is still very much active, with vents spewing sulphur gases and a famous mudpool at the base of the cone, in which tourists wallow. The health benefits of such a dip are controversial; personally, I am not an advocate.

Irazú, Costa Rica

Irazú is the highest of Costa Rica's several active volcanoes, rising to 3,432 metres above sea level. It is a large, and potentially very dangerous, stratovolcano but also a major tourist attraction. A road takes tourists up to the summit crater, from where a short walk rewards them with a view of the volcano's picturesque green crater-lake. Irazú has a history of violent eruptions, often of the explosive Vulcanian type. Since records began in 1723, Irazú has erupted six times, with some eruptions lasting years: the last major eruption started in 1963 and continued until 1965. Although its eruptions play havoc with agriculture, its ash has also helped keep Costa Rica's Central Valley fertile.

PARASOLS AND APPEASEMENT

The Irazú eruption caused havoc in San José and a national emergency was declared on 22 March 1963. The local people came up with all kinds of ideas to stop the ash fall: one engineer suggested building a giant parasol over Irazú's crater and a shaman performed ritual dances on the volcano. People suggested throwing a number of things into the crater, ranging from flowers and crucifixes to virgins and even mothers-in-law.

There had been small explosions since August 1962 but they had not caused much alarm; Irazú's sudden eruption on 9 March 1963 came as a surprise. Ash from the explosion mixed with the waters of the several rivers that have their sources on the Irazú massif to create a mudflow that, during the night, coursed down the Reventado River, destroying at least 300 homes and killing twenty people. On 12 March just as the country was preparing for a visit by the US President, John F Kennedy, Irazú's explosions became far more intense. Great clouds of ash obscured the normally blue sky, torn by occasional lightning flashes as the volcano continued to rumble. Winds blew the ash in drifts towards the country's capital, San José, where it covered everything; sweeping machines had to be brought in from the US to clear the streets. Bombs and smaller fragments of lava fell nearer to the volcano but, happily, no one was killed. Irazú continued to spew ash (most heavily between 17 July and 23 November) and the eruption went on until 1965, with explosions sending columns of steam, gas and ash up to 500 metres above the crater.

Mount Pelée, Martinique

Peléean eruptions can be extremely destructive. The eruption that gave its name to this type of activity, the 1902 eruption of Mount Pelée on Martinique, is a particularly tragic example. This eruption completely destroyed the lovely town of St Pierre, the 'Paris of the Lesser Antilles', and killed some 30,000 people. If the event shocked the world, it also served to boost the study of volcanoes, as scientists strove to understand what had happened and if the eruption could have been predicted. Eventually, it led to the formation of the Hawaii Volcano Observatory.

Mount Pelée is a stratovolcano, rising to 1,397 metres above sea level. It dominates the north-western part of Martinique and is a magnificent backdrop to the present-day town of St Pierre. Only two eruptions from Mount Pelée have been documented: the disastrous eruption of 1902–4 and the less violent eruption of 1929–30. Ironically, European colonisation of the island began in 1635, just a few years after the previous eruption; therefore, although the local people knew the volcano was potentially active, its 1902 reawakening met with disbelief.

The first sign that Mount Pelée was stirring came in 1889, when the volcano began to emit increased quantities of steam and sulphurous gases, but this activity was largely ignored. In February 1902, the emissions of sulphur dioxide were strong enough to be noticeable in St Pierre, killing birds and tarnishing silver. Small earthquakes began to be felt on 22 April, and a day later, steam was seen rising from the volcano's summit. The first explosion came on 25 April an ash cloud rose above the volcano, showering its slopes with fine ash. Although the citizens of St Pierre were worried, they were much more concerned about the upcoming elections for a representative to the legislature. The elections were held on 27 April but the winning candidate's margin of victory was so narrow that a new election had to be scheduled. The chosen date was Sunday, 11 May.

On 2 May the volcanic activity became strong enough to worry residents. There were explosions, rumblings and a glow over the volcano. Crops and livestock on the flanks of the volcano were dying; dead fish floated on the sea's surface. A farmer and some of his farmhands were killed, caught in a mudflow from the volcano. Ashfall over the town of Le Prêcheur, close to the summit crater, was so heavy that life was made miserable for its residents. A few residents of St Pierre realised the seriousness of the situation and fled, ironically just as refugees from the countryside began to pour into the city. St Pierre was covered with fine ash, drinking water was running low and food was becoming scarce. It is amazing that more citizens did not leave but Martinique's governor, Louis Mouttet, desperate to hold the election, was quick to reassure the population that there was no danger. His only action was to set up a Commission of Enquiry to report on the volcano's activity, due to publish its findings on 7 May.

On 5 May things took a turn for the worse. The dried-up bed of the Blanche River was suddenly flooded by a hot mudflow, probably created by water rushing out of the lake in the volcano's crater. The mudflow surged over a sugar mill, covering it with some three metres of mud and killing the owner and twenty-two workers, and rushed on to the sea, creating a small tsunami.

People watched in disbelief as the sea's edge drew back some thirty metres, before rushing inland, devastating a low-lying coastal area. Twenty-eight children drowned when the tsunami wave hit an orphanage and sixty-eight people died in the mulatto quarter. From the capital, Fort-de-France, the governor issued reassurances and encouraged people to remain in St Pierre.

The flooding in the Blanche River continued, breaking the telegraph cable between St Pierre and the island of St Lucia. On 6 May the governor arrived in St Pierre with his wife, to reassure residents that there was no danger. On the morning of Wednesday, 7 May a great cloud first rose above the volcano's summit, then descended as a *nuée ardente* towards the settlement of Fond Corre which, fortunately, had been evacuated. In those days, the dangers of *nuées ardentes* were not really understood; the residents of St Pierre actually felt more optimistic, because it had diminished the height of the cloud above the summit. The Commission of Enquiry released its report, saying that St Pierre was not in danger. In the afternoon, the explosions started again and the Roxelane River, which runs through St Pierre, flooded with muddy water. In the evening, incandescent columns of gas and ash could be seen rising above the volcano.

The moment of doom finally came at 7:50am on Thursday, 8 May Ascension Day, heralded by a loud explosion and a black cloud that rapidly rushed towards St Pierre. The *nuée ardente* engulfed the city, killing nearly all its residents, including the governor and most members of the Commission of Enquiry. The *nuée* left little standing in St Pierre and demolished an area of nearly sixty square kilometres to the west and south-west of the summit crater. The destruction spread to the harbour; the passengers and crew of eighteen vessels were among its victims. In all, some 29,000 people perished. Only two people from the city survived: one, Leon Compère, a shoemaker, was able to run away on the road to St Dennis. The other, Auguste Cyparis, a black man who had been sent to prison convicted of assault and battery, became a celebrity. Shortly before the eruption, Cyparis had tried to escape and, as punishment, had been confined in a dungeon that had only a small window above ground. That dungeon saved his life. On 11 May rescuers heard his cries for help: although badly burned, he had survived. Cyparis recovered and later joined Barnum and Bailey's Circus as 'The Prisoner of St Pierre'.

That was not the end of the eruption: on 20 May the volcano sent another *nuée* towards St Pierre but this time no lives were lost. Other explosions and *nuées* followed, culminating, on 30 August in the largest. This *nuée* devastated an area of about 115 square kilometres, mostly to the south and east of the volcano, destroyed several villages and claimed more than 1,000 lives. After that, the activity subsided and the explosions eventually ceased at the end of September.

As is common with this type of eruption, a pasty lava dome was slowly building up within the crater, although Pelée's was a spine rather than a classic dome. The extrusion began in July and continued for several months; during November, the *Spine of Pelée* grew 230 metres in twenty days. As it grew, it crumbled and then grew some more, attaining its greatest height, towering 340 metres above the crater, on 30 May 1903, just over a year after the tragic destruction of St Pierre. The spine eventually collapsed and the eruption ended in the following year.

Mount Pelée has been quiet since 1904, except for a brief period of dome extrusion between 1929 and 1932. Some collapses of the dome produced small *nuées ardentes* but they were mostly confined to the valley of the Blanche River and no lives were lost. Gradually, St Pierre was rebuilt, as were the villages on the flanks of this very dangerous volcano. These days, Mount Pelée is well-monitored and the local people know that, if the mountain wakes up again, they must be ready to evacuate.

The eruption of Mount Pelée contributed much to the science of volcanology. The French geologist, Albert Lacroix, was one of the first to study the eruption, amassing considerable amounts of information that helped reconstruct the event. With the benefit of Lacroix's and later studies, we now know that St Pierre was not destroyed by a conventional *nuée ardente*, as that would have buried the town under rubble; although the city was certainly obliterated, the ground was covered with only a few centimetres of ash. St Pierre was probably destroyed by a thin, extensive, rapidly moving and ground-hugging pyroclastic surge. Surges have a lower density than pyroclastic flows and are not confined by topography in the way that denser *nuées ardentes* are. It is common for Peléean eruptions to unleash both surges and *nuées*; some studies suggest that the denser part of the *nuée* went down the Blanche River, where a thicker accumulation of coarse deposits can be seen. It seems likely that St Pierre was either destroyed by a combination of blast and pyroclastic surge or by the lateral component of a *nuée ardente* that rushed towards the city. Either way, the consequences were deadly and will not be forgotten.

Mount Lamington, Papua New Guinea

Mount Lamington is an andesitic stratovolcano that rises 1,680 metres above the coastal plain, topped by a 1.3-kilometre-wide summit crater containing a lava dome. Its flanks are dissected by radial valleys, including a prominent, broad avalanche valley that extends north from the breached crater. Before its devastating eruption of 1951, the forested peak was not even known to be a volcano.

The first signs of trouble occurred on 15 January, with seismic activity and an ash plume rising above the volcano. The eruption started in earnest on 21 January, when a violent blast blew away a large part of the northern side of the mountain and *nuées ardentes* poured down its flanks. The area of extreme damage extended some twelve kilometres from the mountain but people up to fourteen kilometres away were killed by the blast or burned to death. The zone of devastation was strongly influenced by topography: the damage was greater to the north-east. In the town of Higaturu, ten kilometres to the north of the crater, many people died. Only one house survived and even then, it was moved some 4.5 metres north by the force of the flow. Earthquakes and explosions continued throughout February, hampering the progress of the rescue. On 5 March, an explosion threw large pieces of the volcanic dome over three kilometres and unleashed a *nuée* that reached fourteen kilometres from the summit. The eruption eventually ended in 1956, after the growth of a 560-metre-high lava dome in the summit crater.

The terrifying eruption killed some 3,000 people and caused considerable damage. However, much was also learned, particularly from the work of the volcanologist George A Taylor, who carefully documented the activity. He is credited with saving lives by letting rescue parties know when it was safe to go into the area. Taylor's observations provided particularly valuable insights into the behaviour of *nuées ardentes*. He noted that, although the flow predominantly ran radially away from the crater, there were local deviations that were not associated with topography. The flow toppled most of the trees in the zone of devastation; Taylor observed that nearly all fell pointing away from the crater except at Higaturu, where there was an area in which the trees fell at right angles to and opposite the predominant flow direction. He concluded this was the result of vortices generated when a tongue thrust ahead of the main front of the flow. Such vortices create not only local variations in direction but also locally higher velocities resulting from turbulence. Perhaps the best-known part of the analysis of the eruption was the use of a severely deformed flagpole at Higaturu Hospital to estimate the velocity of the *nuée ardente*. An engineering analysis of the flagpole, using fluid dynamics and material properties, concluded that the velocity was probably no greater than forty-five metres per second and certainly considerably less than ninety metres per second.

The detailed analysis of this eruption also showed some effects that were hard to explain, such as the uneven distribution of kinetic energy and temperatures. Some people survived while others around them did not; some trees were only lightly charred while others were heavily burned, and so on. Observing the patterns of charring and other temperature effects, Taylor concluded that the temperatures were much lower than those at Pelée in 1902. Although Higaturu was approximately the same distance from its volcano as St Pierre from Mount Pelée, temperatures there were not high enough to ignite or char trees. These effects, and others, led him to conclude that temperatures of around 200°C had lasted one to two minutes. These were important conclusions, as they showed that *nuées ardentes* can vary greatly not only in their overall behaviour but also locally. Lamington has remained mostly quiet since 1956 but worryingly, on 21 December 2000 and 17 February 2001, the volcano underwent several hours of very high seismic activity. However, so far, Lamington has not offered a repeat performance of the 1951 eruption.

Viewing Vulcanian and Peléean eruptions

Vulcanian eruptions can be mild and continuous enough to become tourist attractions but visitors need to be a long way away from the volcano to be sure of safety. Peléean eruptions are even less suitable for tourists: their *nuées ardentes* are one of the most deadly of volcanic products; those caught in their deadly path have an almost-zero chance of survival. Even their rare survivors suffer severe burns. However, if the eruption is at its end, during the dome or spine building phase, it can be relatively safe to climb to the crater and view the dome or spine from a vantage point. Most visitors, such as the many who still visit St Pierre, are content to see the aftermath of these eruptions.

6

Plinian and Ultraplinian eruptions: the great catastrophes

Plinian eruptions, and their more violent siblings, the Ultraplinians, have extremely powerful explosions that eject great volumes of fragmented magma over hundreds of square kilometres. Some of the most infamous, destructive and death-dealing eruptions in history have been of these types. The eruption cloud, coming out at speeds of hundreds of metres per second, can reach far above the volcano – a height of forty-five kilometres above ground has been recorded, well into the stratosphere. Although much of the ash falls back down, some stays in the atmosphere, scattering sunlight; Plinian eruptions create vivid, red sunsets around the world. The dust clouds can be a serious hazard to aviation, as shown most recently by the 2010 eruption of Eyjafjallajökull in Iceland. In the months following the Pinatubo eruption in 1991, dust damaged the engines of nine passenger jet planes badly enough for them to need emergency landings. Since then, a better system has been developed to warn aviation of the dangers from ash clouds. However, the most profound global effect of Plinian eruptions is their effect on the climate (see Chapter 2).

Fortunately, Plinian eruptions are rare, occurring perhaps a few times a century. Recent examples include Mount St Helens in 1980 and Pinatubo in 1991, but perhaps the most famous

Plinian eruption was the one that caused this type of eruption to be named after a person rather than a location: the eruption of Vesuvius in 79 CE. The man thus honoured was Pliny the Younger, who witnessed the events and gave the world its first scientific description of a volcanic eruption.

Plinian eruptions are renowned because they are so destructive, creating considerable damage with ash and pumice falls and pyroclastic surges and flows. When the vast quantities of ash mix with rainfall or melted ice, the resulting mudflows can be devastating. Plinian eruptions can destroy the volcanoes themselves: the quantity of magma ejected by the volcano can be so large that the magma reservoir is completely drained, leaving the top of the volcano unsupported, which then caves in to form a crater or caldera. Crater Lake in Oregon, US, was formed after the prehistoric eruption of Mount Mazama, which was largely destroyed by its own eruption.

Vesuvius, Italy, 79 CE

Vesuvius is the most famous of all Plinian eruptions. Who has not heard the story of the overwhelming of the sinful Roman cities of Pompeii and Herculaneum by the unexpected eruption of Mount Vesuvius? Contrary to popular belief, Vesuvius did send out warnings; if the Romans had known then what we know now, they would have fled and been saved. In fact, many did leave during the first, non-lethal, stages of Vesuvius's activity. Much of what we know about this eruption comes from the eyewitness account of Pliny the Younger, contained in a letter sent to the historian, Tacitus. Marrying the geological evidence from the various layers of deposits and the eyewitness account from Pliny has made it possible to reconstruct the sequence of events amazingly well.

The eruption began with a brief but violent explosive phase, some time between the late night of 23 August and the early morning of the following day. This phase produced a relatively small volume of fine ash which fell on the eastern slopes of the volcano. Although the residents must have been alarmed, most did not leave. The main population centres near the volcano were Pompeii, located about eight kilometres to the south-east, and Herculaneum, about six kilometres to the west, along with a number of smaller communities, including the royal villa of Oplontis and the town of Stabiae, about fourteen kilometres to the south-east (the present-day town of Castellammare di Stabia). Much further away, about thirty-two kilometres across the Bay of Naples, was Misenum, where Pliny the Younger lived with his mother and uncle, Pliny the Elder. The older man was a keen student of nature as well as a statesman and Admiral in command of the Roman fleet at Misenum.

On 24 August at 1pm, the two men watched the eruption column rising above the volcano; its lower portion was narrow, broadening as it rose until it resembled a Mediterranean stone pine tree. Within minutes, the cloud rose to about fiften kilometres high. Pliny the Elder decided to take a ship into the bay, to take a closer look at the strange phenomenon. Just as he was leaving his house, he received an urgent plea for help from a noble lady, Rectina. The lady was staying at her 'villa under the mountain'; its location is now unknown but it was probably within reach of the first ashfall. Pliny the Elder set out on a rescue mission.

Because of the wind direction, Pompeii suffered most intensely. For seven hours, white pumice fell and accumulated over Pompeii; the fragments grew larger, to fist-size, and dense ashfall pelted the city. The fragments crashed to the ground at speeds estimated to be up to fifty metres per second, probably directly injuring or killing some people. The pumice accumulated at about fifteen centimetres an hour, causing roofs to collapse under its weight. Many residents left the city, even though travelling was difficult as the eruption cloud obscured the sun: the region around the volcano was in total darkness that afternoon. One can only imagine how terrified the residents must have been.

They had no idea that Vesuvius was an active volcano; the mountain had been so quiet for so long that its summit was covered in vegetation. During the evening, the composition of the erupting magma changed: grey pumice now started to fall over the city and continued to accumulate for five hours. The eruption column rose to thirty-three kilometres high, but the volcano had not unleashed its worst.

Very early on 25 August, Vesuvius produced the first of six *nuées ardentes* that continued to flow for the next seven hours, each separating into a slower-moving pyroclastic flow and a less dense, more turbulent surge, travelling at up to a hundred kilometres per hour. There was no time to flee; most people killed during the eruption were engulfed by surges. The destruction caused by the first pyroclastic surge was most dramatic in Herculaneum. The city had suffered little ashfall, perhaps less than a centimetre, in the previous twelve hours. Some citizens had left: they were the lucky ones. The remaining residents, watching the volcano throughout the night, probably saw the surge coming down towards them. It is estimated that it took less than ten minutes to travel the six kilometres from the volcano to the city. People ran to the waterfront, seeking shelter inside the arched chambers of the boat houses. The pyroclastic surge entered the city at about 1am, engulfing the people sheltering in the chambers and huddled on the beach. The pyroclastic flow reached the city shortly after. Because of the higher density of the flow and Herculaneum's relatively high position, it did not go through the city but was diverted down a valley along its southern edge and onto the beach in front of the public baths, covering the surge deposits before entering the sea.

Before 1982, only ten skeletons had been found in Herculaneum; historians assumed that most of the residents had fled. Unfortunately, this was not the case: the 1982 excavations at the waterfront discovered several hundred skeletons on the beach and inside the chambers, covered by pyroclastic surge deposits. However, most of the 4,500 residents appear to have escaped.

It is thought they fled to Naples and settled in what became known as the Herculaneum Quarter.

Two other pyroclastic flows and surges were unleashed during the night but neither reached Pompeii, where many people were still alive. However, at about 6:30am on 25 August, things took a turn for the worse and a heavy fall of dark pumice pelted the city. The fourth pyroclastic surge came at about 7:30am, overwhelming Pompeii. Although most of the residents had fled, about 2,000 people, ten per cent of the population, are thought to have died there. Shortly after, an even larger surge came down and enveloped the city once more.

VESUVIUS: A TIMELINE

The account by Pliny the Younger and studies of the various layers of deposits from the eruption have allowed volcanologists to reconstruct this ancient eruption in detail.

24 August

1pm:	first fall of white ash east of Vesuvius
1:30pm:	ash pumice falls to the south-east of the volcano
5:30pm:	roofs of houses in Pompeii begin to collapse
8pm:	grey pumice begins to fall

25 August

1am:	first pyroclastic surge reaches Herculaneum
6:30am:	pyroclastic surge reaches north wall of Pompeii
7am:	pyroclastic surge comes within the walls of Pompeii
8am:	largest surge, devastation

By this time, Pliny the Elder had arrived at Stabiae. The previous afternoon, he had been forced to give up his rescue mission; the heavy ashfall and lumps of pumice floating on the ocean made sailing near the south-western coast of the volcano impossible, but at Stabiae, although the fall was heavy, conditions were manageable. Around 8am, the sixth and largest surge advanced towards Stabiae. Pliny the Elder perished, but the exact cause of his death is unknown. One possibility is that he died from heart failure. Pliny the Younger's last account refers to the surge as a 'tongue of fire' that caused his uncle's death. He says his uncle had a weak constitution and that he collapsed, choking in the dust cloud, in the arms of his two slaves (who survived). From the sequence of deposits, it is known that several more surges occurred over the following days or weeks. The final phase of the eruption was a series of small explosions caused by the interaction of the remaining magma with groundwater. Pliny the Younger's home, Misenum, did not escape the devastation. Severe earthquakes toppled its buildings and Pliny and his mother left the city.

In the mere two days of the eruption, some four cubic kilometres of magma were released and an area of approximately 300 square kilometres around the volcano was consumed. Vesuvius became synonymous with volcanic catastrophe. Although it was not the most powerful eruption in historic times, the event became symbolic of the power and tragedy a volcano can unleash. What is perhaps most frightening is that Vesuvius erupts in cycles, each lasting several centuries, with the initial eruption being the most violent. The last cycle ended in 1944. Since then, Vesuvius has enjoyed its longest period of repose for some 350 years. Will Vesuvius erupt again and, if so, how devastating will the next eruption be? Or, as some argue, has the volcano finally become extinct? The answers to these questions are unknown but they affect the lives of the millions of people who still live in Vesuvius's shadow.

Mount St Helens, USA, 1980

Mount St Helens, in Washington State in the US, became one of the world's most famous volcanoes when it erupted in May 1980.

The eruption had a relatively low death toll compared to many other Plinian eruptions; what made this tragedy stick in people's minds was that Mount St Helens was being monitored by the best equipment and some of the top volcanologists in the world. The volcano sent out plenty of warning signs and a wide area was evacuated, yet it was not wide enough. There was an unknown factor: the volcanologists expected the blast to go vertically; instead, it went sideways. The surprise came partly because the eruption patterns of St Helens were not well known. The mountain had been quiet for decades and its eruptions in historic times were not especially violent; the last major activity, recorded in 1857, did not cause widespread damage.

The 1980 eruption first sent out warnings on 16 March, in the form of a series of small earthquakes, noted only by seismographs. On 20 March, a magnitude 4.2 earthquake again warned that something was happening inside the mountain but it caused no alarm to the local people as, apparently, no one felt it. Earthquakes became more frequent during the following week; the scientists knew that magma might be moving up. On 27 March, an explosion sent a plume of ash and steam about two kilometres above the volcano and opened a new crater, some seventy-five metres wide, inside the summit crater. No new magma had yet arrived at the surface; the explosion was phreatic (caused by the interaction of the rising hot magma with water and snow). It was clear that St Helens was beginning a new phase in its volcanic career: it meant business.

Phreatic explosions continued over the following weeks, ejecting ash and steam in bursts lasting from a few seconds to tens of minutes. Still there was no new magma; all the ash came from the old summit dome. Another new crater was formed; later, the two new craters merged. Several avalanches of ash-blackened snow and ice streaked down the mountain's flanks and earthquakes shook the area. Scientists from the US Geological Survey settled in for what they thought might be a long watch, civic officials prepared evacuation plans and journalists, photographers and tourists arrived from all over the world.

All this time, magma moved up inside St Helens, causing large and rapid deformation of the ground. The magma heated the groundwater and more phreatic explosions happened at the summit. The pressure of the magma moving inside St Helens threatened to wedge the mountain apart: about 2,500 metres up the north flank, an ominous bulge grew at the alarming rate of 1.5 metres a day. Even if there were no eruption, Forsyth Glacier, at the site of the bulge, could slide down and race into Spirit Lake, which lay below. Officials realised the danger and established a five-mile 'red zone' around the summit. Some residents were far from happy: Harry Truman, an eighty-three-year-old Spirit Lake resident, completely refused to move. Others went but complained that they needed to retrieve more of their possessions. On Saturday, 17 May, the local police escorted residents into the red zone to retrieve their belongings.

At 8:32am on Sunday, 18 May, a young volcanologist, David Johnston, on duty at an observation post about ten kilometres north of the volcano, made a frantic call to his fellow scientists: 'Vancouver! Vancouver! This is it!' Johnston's post, located on a ridge, had been considered safe: no one had predicted that the unstable, bulging north flank would collapse, triggering a series of events that led to the deaths of fifty-seven people, many of whom were outside the red zone. The collapse of the flank caused an almost instantaneous release of the high-temperature, high-pressure steam which had been dissolved in the magma that formed the bulge. The avalanche uncorked those gases and unleashed an enormous lateral blast of rock, gases and ash that sped downhill in a deadly fan, devastating an area of some 600 square kilometres, mostly to the north of the volcano, within moments. The blast – which came seconds after the avalanche was triggered – had an initial velocity of about 350 kilometres per hour but it soon increased to some 1,100 kilometres per hour. The volcanic debris in the blast included the first new magma, released from the magma dome. The magnitude of the blast was estimated to be about 500 times greater than that of the Hiroshima atomic bomb. Everything in its path was blown away.

Shortly after the lateral blast, another strong explosion created a column of gas and ash that rose more than nineteen kilometres above the volcano. The winds took the cloud towards the east and north-east; when it reached the towns of Yakima at 9.45am and Spokane at 11.45am, it was dense enough to block the sunlight. Destructive mudflows began a few minutes after the blast, as the hot material in the debris avalanche and ash from the erupting column mixed with the snow and ice on the mountain's flanks. The mudflows travelled up to 150 kilometres per hour, flowing down both forks of the Toutle River. Even after travelling tens of kilometres, the mud remained hot. The mudflow over-ran two logging camps, killing at least three people, before it reached the town of Toutle, about forty kilometres away from the mountain, where it destroyed everything close to the river. More than a thousand people were evacuated from the town. The mud and debris eventually reached the Columbia River, reducing the depth of its navigational channel from twelve metres to four metres and causing chaos as river traffic was forced to a halt. The ashfall closed roads and grounded planes; some 10,000 travellers were stranded.

Pyroclastic flows probably formed soon after the blast but the first confirmed flow occurred just after noon, followed by another seventeen flows in the following five hours. The largest flows started with upwelling of material, mostly pumice, in the crater, which flowed northward, escaping through a breach in the crater wall. Although pyroclastic flows had been a major concern, they did little damage beyond that already done by the blast and mudflows. The eruption began to subside the next day, by which time the ash cloud had spread across the USA; ashfall affected an area of about 57,000 square kilometres. The mountain suffered major damage: a giant amphitheatre now dominated the northern side and the crater rim stood some 900 metres lower than before the eruption.

Since the eruption, a dome has grown inside the crater. This has caused some concern recently; after twenty years of relative quiescence, small explosions have been recorded. Fortunately, Plinian eruptions are rare; St Helens will probably settle down for a while before the next one. The lessons learnt at St Helens were later used to predict hazards and minimise loss of life during the 1991 eruption of Pinatubo, in the Philippines.

Krakatau, Indonesia, 1883

This Ultraplinian eruption is one of the most infamous of all time: the 1883 Krakatau eruption was more violent than the 79 CE eruption of Vesuvius and caused a much greater loss of life. It has been the subject of several books and even a film, entitled *Krakatoa, East of Java* (despite the volcano being west of Java and having the accepted spelling of Krakatau). It is estimated that 36,420 people lost their lives in the 1883 eruption, many in the enormous tsunami that engulfed the low-lying coastal areas in the Sunda Straits. The effects of the eruption were felt all over the world and the island of Krakatau was almost completely destroyed.

Before 1883, the volcano lay dormant; an uninhabited, densely vegetated island between Java and Sumatra, about nine kilometres long and four kilometres wide. It was formed from a series of volcanic cones; one of these, Perboewatan, was known to have erupted in 1680–1 but that had been a relatively mild eruption. Active volcanoes are so common in Indonesia that the island of Krakatau seemed unremarkable. Everything started to change on 20 May 1883, when Perboewatan came to life, shooting a column of ash and steam some eleven kilometres high. The explosions were heard in Batavia (Jakarta), 155 kilometres away, and ash fell on southern Sumatra. These fireworks did not cause any great concern; sight-seers came by steamer to get a closer look. On 27 May, they reported a crater on Perboewatan, about one kilometre wide, exploding every five to ten minutes. By mid-June, the top of Perboewatan had been blown off and two other eruption vents had started exploding. Still there was no great concern. By mid-July, banks of pumice were seen floating in the Sunda Straits. A government surveyor, HJG Ferzenaar, is the last person known to have visited the island; on 11 August, he reported that the eruption appeared to have subsided, at least temporarily, that all the forests had been burnt and that the whole island was fuming and covered in ash.

In the third week of August, the explosions became bigger and more frequent, ejecting huge, dark columns of gas and ash, some twenty-five kilometres high, which could be seen from Java and Sumatra. Krakatau was getting ready to unleash its worst: on Sunday, 26 August, around noon, the eruption reached its peak and continued furiously for fifty hours. The most extreme outburst came in the morning of Monday, 27 August, when the sound of the volcano's explosions reached further than any noise known before; the column of gas and ash towered fifty kilometres above the volcano. The worst effect was a consequence of the explosions occurring near, or under, the sea: catastrophic tsunamis. The gigantic waves, thirty metres high, swept away everything on the low-lying areas of the Sunda Straits, crashing into shores, destroying whole villages and drowning many thousands of people.

Although the eruption of Tambora, also in Indonesia, earlier that century was larger in volcanological terms, Krakatau was the eruption felt around the world. Noises from the larger explosions, described as sounding like muffled gunfire, were heard as far away as Rodriguez, in the Indian Ocean – 4,653 kilometres away. The tsunami's effects were felt in the Pacific and Indian Oceans: in Auckland, New Zealand, 7,767 kilometres from Krakatau, an unusual two-metre-high wave was recorded. Pumice banks choked parts of the Sunda Straits until December, a gruesome sight, as clusters of corpses floated among the rocks. One pumice accumulation floated over 8,000 kilometres and reached South Africa.

The eruption ejected massive amounts of ash and gases, forming a sulphuric aerosol cloud in the stratosphere. The aerosol travelled around the world, completing its first circuit on 9 September and its second on 22 September, creating brilliant sunsets that inspired painters such as the well-known English artist, William Ashcroft.

Krakatau stayed dormant until 1927, when Anak ('child of') Krakatau erupted in the seafloor hollow created by the earlier eruption. Little Anak has erupted fairly regularly since then, but so far its activity has been mild and mostly Strombolian. We can only hope the child will not grow up to be like its parent.

Santorini, Greece, around 1600 BCE

Santorini, these days a lively holiday spot, was the site of one of the most catastrophic eruptions of historic times. Known as the Minoan eruption, it occurred some time between 1650 and 1600 BCE and has been much studied and much debated, particularly because of its possible connection to the decline of the Minoan civilisation. Santorini today is a series of islands surrounding a sunken caldera. In the middle is Nea Kameni, still an active volcano, but its eruptions have been of the Strombolian type and have not posed any great danger to the residents of Santorini.

It is not known how long the 1600 BCE eruption lasted but the sequence of events has been reconstructed from excavations at the Minoan city of Akrotiri and from the study of the deposits the eruption left behind, including the many layers on the tall cliffs that define the walls of the caldera. It is known that the activity started with earthquakes powerful enough to cause the residents to leave the island: no bodies or precious artefacts have ever been found. Evidence from excavations and archaeological studies shows that the residents came back at some stage and started repairing the damage to their buildings. This suggests that the earthquakes stopped, at least for a little while. Then the people fled again, either because of more earthquakes or because of explosions heralding the beginning of the eruption. These were probably fairly small phreatic eruptions, which gave people time to get away. Fine pumice fell over the whole island, leaving a layer about two centimetres thick. This layer shows signs of oxidation in places, which further indicates that the eruption must have stopped for a time. It is lucky that the residents did not return after the first phase of the eruption stopped, because the next phase was much worse: explosions showered the island with enough pumice to create deposits over a metre thick.

The next event in the eruption – the true Plinian eruption – was utterly catastrophic. The eruption column reached thirty-six kilometres high, ejecting huge quantities of ash into the atmosphere. Pumice fragments showered the island, creating a layer over thirty metres thick in places. Huge boulders were hurled around the island, some reaching Akrotiri, where they can be seen today in the excavated city. Next came pyroclastic surges. The surge deposits lie on top of the thick pumice layer but some pumice fragments are mixed in, meaning that pumice fall continued throughout. After several hours of activity, seawater entered the vent: the caldera began to collapse and fractures spread from the vent area to the north-west and south-west. The seawater and hot magma mixed, causing violent explosions and sending powerful torrents of water, ash and lava fragments and mudflows strong enough to carry blocks of lava ten metres across racing from the volcano.

Pyroclastic flows came next, at temperatures of between 200°C and 400°C, which created deposits of ignimbrites up to forty metres thick. Within and over the ignimbrites lie deposits of flood breccias (made up of fragmented rocks), thought to have formed when the pyroclastic flows ripped up portions of the mudflow deposits, smearing out the debris. Flash floods probably started soon after, as the ignimbrite deposits near Akrotiri have been eroded and covered by alluvial deposits, formed by water carrying soil and sediment.

It is not known how long the Minoan eruption lasted but it was extremely powerful, discharging about 30 cubic kilometres of magma and sending ash as far as western Turkey. The island was torn apart and lost over eighty square kilometres of its original area. It remained uninhabited for some time after the eruption; pottery fragments suggest that there was some re-settlement by the end of the thirteenth century BCE. The Lacedonians settled on the largest island in the ninth century BCE, naming it Thera, in honour of their leader, Theras, and it has been inhabited ever since. Since about 197 BCE, small eruptions have continued, during which dacitic magma has slowly leaked out and built a shield, mostly underwater. The islands of Nea Kameni and Palea Kameni are the surface tips of this shield, which is about 3.5 kilometres in diameter and 500 metres above the submerged caldera floor.

The Minoan eruption has captured people's imaginations. Did it cause the downfall of the Minoan civilisation? This question has been fiercely debated but most scholars agree that the Minoans were already in decline by the time of the eruption. Although the main centre of Minoan civilisation was in Crete, not Santorini, Crete suffered effects from the eruption, including earthquakes. Indeed, life and trade across the Mediterranean must have been affected by the catastrophe: it was certainly powerful enough to have vast effects and could have inspired legends. The large quantities of ash injected into the atmosphere must have had significant consequences, both local and global, probably triggering global cooling in a similar way to other powerful Plinian eruptions. The eruption has even been linked to Egypt's plague of darkness and the parting of the Red Sea. Drifting ash could have inspired the Biblical accounts of the plague of darkness, although the parting of the Red Sea is harder to explain; it has been proposed to be a tsunami caused by the eruption but no clear evidence has been found. There are also problems with the linking of dates, as the dates of the Exodus are poorly defined.

Was Santorini Plato's 'Lost Atlantis', the great civilisation suddenly and violently destroyed by the sea around 1500 BCE? This seems unlikely, even assuming that Plato's account was based on real events. Santorini is a poor candidate for Atlantis: its naval power and standard of civilisation were well below those of the mighty Atlantis and Akrotiri was largely destroyed by and completely abandoned before the eruption. Yet the myth remains. The Greek archaeologist, Spyridon Marinatos, has proposed a sensible explanation for this persistent legend: that the story came to Plato from Egyptian priests some 900 years after the eruption. Because so many centuries had gone by, it is possible that the priests confused the destruction of a civilisation (Minoan Crete) with the 'sinking' of an island (Santorini). However, given its size, it is perhaps not surprising that the eruption of Santorini could have inspired the story of the destruction of an island empire 'in a single day and night'.

Viewing Plinian and Ultraplinian eruptions

There is really no sense in trying to see such eruptions up close: they are extremely dangerous and it is very hazardous to approach a volcano that is showing signs of having such a violent eruption. It is best to get away, comply with the advice of local authorities and come back later to see the aftermath of the eruptions, which can last for centuries. Visitors today enjoy seeing Pompeii, Herculaneum and Akrotiri and learning about the eruptions of Vesuvius and Santorini so long ago. They come to Mount St Helens to see much more recently devastated areas and to Anak Krakatau to see the child that will hopefully never become as violent as its parent.

7

The tricky killers: mudflows and degassing

Volcanoes can be lethal even without an eruption: sometimes a volcano kills silently or subtly, with little or no new magma ejected. Although rare, such disasters are reminders that the study of volcanoes and their hazards is neither straightforward nor, necessarily, predictable. The tragedy of Nevado del Ruiz occurred because the local people could not know that a relatively small eruption several kilometres away would kill them during the night. More bizarre – and fortunately rare – was the deadly degassing of Lake Nyos in 1986, which silently killed an entire village. Perhaps both disasters could have been prevented if we had known more about these strange phenomena.

Nevado del Ruiz, Colombia, 1985

On 13 November 1985, the majestic Nevado del Ruiz volcano caused one of the worst natural disasters of the century, killing about 23,000 people. The volcano didn't hit its victims with a single drop of magma; they were claimed by mudflows that formed when magma melted part of the mountain's ice cap. The mudflows rushed down the mountainside and eventually overwhelmed the town of Armero, lying some sixty kilometres from the summit crater. News of the disaster made headlines around the world at a time when few people had ever heard of this volcano. The eruption that caused the tragedy was a relatively small one but, because of the snow-cap and the location of Armero, it was overwhelmingly deadly.

Perhaps the most tragic aspect is that the mudflows could have been predicted. Nevado ('snow-capped') del Ruiz, like many high volcanoes where snow and ice persist on the summit, poses a real danger of triggering mudflows. It had happened before, in 1595 and 1845, but those mudflows had caused relatively few deaths: the 1595 mudflow killed 636 people, mostly from the local Guali tribe, and the 1845 mudflow claimed about 1,000 victims and destroyed the town of Ambalema. The town of Armero was built on the deposits of the 1845 mudflow: this is not uncommon; parts of Seattle and Tacoma in Washington State are built on old mudflow deposits from Mount Rainier.

Nevado del Ruiz gave plenty of warning that an eruption was about to happen: fifty-one weeks' warning, with many small earthquakes and even some small phreatic explosions. However, the local government was not particularly organised in its disaster planning and the advice from experts was somewhat contradictory. In the meantime, during the first eight months of 1985, the volcano continued to erupt but the relatively mild activity did not raise very much concern. A scientific commission visited the volcano on 8 July and reported that steam was starting to melt some of the ice. A few seismographs were placed on the volcano to monitor its activity: unfortunately, the data were analysed in the capital, Bogotá, where little local expertise was available. On 11 September, a vigorous explosion sent out a cloud of ash, coating the summit and showering the town of Manizales. The steam melted some of the ice cap, sending a mudflow about twenty-seven kilometres down the valley of the River Azufrado. Some local officials were concerned but evacuation plans were left to individual provinces, with no central co-ordination. In September, a national newspaper, *El Tiempo*, drew attention to Armero for the first time, reporting that in 1984, a landslide had partly dammed the River Lagunillas, only twelve kilometres away. An eruption could break the dam and unleash vast quantities of water onto the town. The president of the Red Cross warned that Armero 'might disappear' if an eruption formed a large mud-flow. The Mayor of Armero, to his credit, tried to get government help to deal with the dam but his request was not granted. Again, scientific advice was conflicting: some scientists did not think the threat was a major one.

The earthquakes died down during October which, in view of what was to come, was unfortunate. Although the volcano was still showing signs of activity, puffing steam up to two kilometres high, the local media and many authorities believed that the danger had been exaggerated. On 7 October a local agency, INGEOMINAS, published a hazard map, but civil unrest in Bogotá meant few copies were produced and its impact was limited. Although one newspaper pointed out that the residents of Armero would have less than two hours to evacuate their town, there were no evacuation plans; no one seemed to know where the people would go, how the evacuation would be organised or by whom or who would pay for it.

The scientists were becoming more concerned. INGEOMINAS published a report based on the seismic activity and used a local newspaper to warn that a larger eruption would melt the ice cap and trigger mudflows, with great danger to Armero and sur-rounding areas. Some government officials did not believe the report, calling it 'too alarming'. A team of Italian volcanologists arrived in mid-October and found the situation very alarming indeed. On 31 October, they reported to the government that the gases escaping from the crater were coming from new magma, which had probably already risen high inside the volcano: a larger eruption was imminent. On 12 November, a team of scientists visited the volcano and saw nothing unusual. They didn't know what was about to unfold.

The next day, 13 November, started quietly but, just after 3pm, a powerful explosion sent ash, wet with rain, as far as fifty kilometres north-east of the volcano. Settlements near rivers coming down from Nevado del Ruiz were warned of probable mudflows. In the late afternoon, ash began falling on Armero but still local officials told residents to stay calm, there was nothing to worry about. At 7pm, the Red Cross representative in Armero was asked to evacuate the town but, by then, ash had stopped falling and the eruption seemed to be over. However, Nevado del Ruiz was not finished. At 9:08pm, the volcano erupted fresh magma for the first time. Hot material scattered over the ice cap, melting part of it. Smouldering ash created a glow above the volcano, explosions scattered ash over the upper slopes and a dozen pyroclastic flows came down but did not reach any towns. By most standards, it was a small eruption: the volume of magma thrown out was only about 0.006 cubic kilometres. Unfortunately, even this small amount was enough to cause deep, rapidly moving, lethal mudflows, with the consistency of wet cement, which picked up speed as they raced down the steep slopes of the volcano and through the river valleys, gathering up ash, soil, ice, snow, vegetation and anything else that was in their way.

One mudflow ran westwards down the River Cauca, engulfing the town of Chinchiná at 10:40pm. Radio stations issued red alert messages but the town could not be completely evacuated. The torrent destroyed three bridges and some 200 houses and killed 1,927 people. Other mudflows spread down other river valleys. The most lethal was the one that formed at about 9:30pm at the head of the River Azufrado, sending a flow of some 48,000 cubic metres a second, with a thirty-metre-high front, roaring at about thirty-six kilometres per hour down the steep, narrow valley.

The people of Armero were indoors, sheltering from the ashy rain pelting the town. It seems that between 9:45pm and 10:30pm, officials in other towns radioed their colleagues in Armero and told them to evacuate: no one knows why this didn't happen. At 11:35pm, the mudflow reached Armero. Most people died within a few minutes, struck by the many boulders carried on the mud. The scene that greeted rescuers the next day was one of unbelievable horror: so many dead; so many others dying before they could be rescued. It was clear that the many warnings had not been heeded. After the disaster, the Colombian Volcanological Observatory was created; these days, Nevado del Ruiz is well monitored. It took 23,000 deaths for its threat to be taken seriously.

Lake Nyos, Cameroon, 1986

Few people, including volcanologists, had heard of Lake Nyos before 1986. Located in the Grassfields area of Cameroon, near the border with Nigeria, the lake is about 1.5 square kilometres in area, about 208 metres deep and lies at an altitude of 1,091 metres. In the rainy seasons, water runs down the valley towards the village of Nyos. In 1986, carbon dioxide gas, rather than water, escaped from the lake. This was a very rare volcanic phenomenon; its cause is still the subject of debate.

Lake Nyos was formed about 400 years ago by explosive volcanic activity that formed a crater. The lake lies over a magma chamber from which volcanic gases escape and filter up towards the floor of the lake. On Thursday, 21 August 1986, at about 4pm, some herdsmen heard gurgling noises from the lake; at about 8pm, some villagers in Cha, six kilometres away from the lake, heard several 'detonation' noises. At about 8:30pm, with almost no warning, a cloudy jet of carbon dioxide and water droplets – about a cubic kilometre in total – emerged from the lake at an estimated speed of about a hundred kilometres per hour. At about 10 pm, the cloud engulfed a group of houses 120 metres above the lake, then began to spread more slowly, as it lost its water. Carbon dioxide is denser than air, so the cloud hugged the ground as it spread downhill at about twenty to fifty kilometres per hour. The cloud, about forty metres high, became an invisible, deadly mass that reached the village of Nyos some time before midnight, suffocating its people as they slept in their beds. In a few hours, the cloud took an estimated 1,742 human lives and the lives of countless animals, including some 6,000 cattle. Nyos was the worst-hit community, although 58 people also died in the village of Cha, some 400 in Subum, fifteen kilometres away from the lake and a few near Koskin, twenty-three kilometres away. At its greatest extent, the cloud covered 34.6 square kilometres.

THE DEADLIEST LAKE IN THE WORLD

Following the 1986 disaster, Lake Nyos was named the 'Deadliest Lake in the World' by the *Guinness Book of Records*. Local mythology agrees with this opinion: the people of Nyos have long held that the lake is deadly. Cameroonian mythology reserves a special category for lakes, which are said to be the homes of ancestors and spirits and sometimes a source of death. According to legend, lakes may rise, sink, explode or even change locations. Some of the local people believe that houses near lakes should be erected on high ground – could this be a case of stories of ancient disaster being passed down the generations?

The next day, a helicopter pilot reported that the colour of the lake had changed from muddy brown to a bright orange with black streaks. There was evidence that water had swept up from the southern part of the lake and stripped a small area down to bare rock. A few days later, scientists measured the water temperature and found that, two metres down, the temperature was 30°C instead of the usual 23°C. Not until mid-September did the water return to its normal temperature. There were two further emissions in the next few months but these were on a much smaller scale and did not cause any deaths. Three explosions from the lake were heard on 30 December; then, after the second gas escape in January 1987, the lake went quiet.

What caused the gas to be released? There are two competing theories: first, that the gas erupted and burst out suddenly from the lake, and second, that the gas came out slowly and became concentrated in the lower layers of the lake; the lake waters then overturned and caused the release of the gas. Uncovering the true explanation is important for preventing future disaster. If a sudden volcanic explosion was responsible for the 1986 disaster, a recurrence would be harder to predict and perhaps impossible to avoid. However, many experts favour the slow release theory, so it makes sense to try to prevent a recurrence by siphoning water from the lower layers of the lake. The gas dissolved in these layers slowly bubbles out of the water as it reaches lower pressures nearer the surface: some gas was successfully removed from the lake by this method in 1995.

8

Geysers and geothermal areas

Geothermal areas are found in many volcanic regions. Two of the most famous are Yellowstone in the western USA, and Rotorua in New Zealand, which are located above the most potentially lethal volcanoes in the world: Yellowstone and Taupo respectively. Their beautiful geysers, colourful hot springs and bubbling mud pots hide the fact that these would be very dangerous places indeed if they were to erupt.

Geothermal areas lie above sizeable magma chambers. The system works like a giant natural boiler, in which the hot magma supplies the heat that turns rainwater into pressurised hot water. The rainwater trickles down from the surface through cracks and fractures and seeps through porous rocks, which soak up the water like a sponge. Heat from the magma chamber below reaches the permeable rock layer and heats the water. Because of the pressure of the water and the rock above it, the water trapped in the permeable rock layer may become superheated, reaching temperatures of over 260°C without boiling. The superheated water is less dense than the cool water that enters the system from above, so it rises towards the surface to form fumaroles, hot springs or geysers.

If the path to the surface is unobstructed and a relatively small amount of water rises through it, the water will boil as the pressure drops and emerge at the surface as a fumarole, or steam vent. Fumaroles are very common in all volcanic regions. If superheated water mixes with cool water on the way up and does not boil, it surfaces as a hot spring or mud pot, depending on whether mud from surrounding rocks has mixed with the rising water. The rocks lining a hot spring readily disintegrate and turn into mud because of the corrosive action of the sulphuric acid formed from hydrogen sulphide in the hot spring water, which is oxidised both by chemical reactions and by primitive types of bacteria, such as *Sulfolobus* species. The appearance of mud pots varies during the year, depending on the amount of rainfall and snow-melt, ranging from 'paint pots' of thin consistency to pasty 'mud volcanoes'. Sometimes, a mud pot dries up completely and reverts to a fumarole. The steam and gases rising from the fumaroles is what makes the pots bubble.

If the hot spring has enough sub-surface water to prevent mud and debris from filling up the depression and the water from boiling away, a thermal pool is formed. The temperature of the water is usually close to boiling point, so it does not become stagnant. The water sometimes appears vividly coloured but it is, in fact, so clear that it absorbs all colours of the spectrum except the blues and greens, much in the same way as oceans and clear lakes. The exact shade of the pool – turquoise, azure or jade-green – depends on the depth and volume of the water. Bacteria and algae thrive at the cooler edges and in the run-off channels of hot springs, adding beautiful orange and yellow tones to the water. Different temperatures of water allow different types of algae and bacteria to grow: in a typical hot spring, the run-off channel is clear near the source, because only a few single-celled bacteria can live in water at about 93°C. As the water gets slightly cooler, thermophilic (warmth-loving) bacteria develop in long, hair-like strands. Further away, as the water cools down to about 75°C, colourful cyanobacteria thrive in microbial mats.

Fumaroles, ordinary hot springs and thermal pools are found in many places throughout the world. Geysers, however, are much rarer. They are a special type of hot spring, characterised by an intermittent discharge of water ejected turbulently, powered by pressure from the gases (mostly steam) rising from below. The way a geyser works is fairly simple but the conditions have to be exactly right. Below a geyser, superheated water rises into pockets of groundwater held under sufficiently great pressure that the water cannot boil. The temperature of the mixing waters rises until a small amount of water boils despite the pressure. The resulting steam, which has a volume much greater than that of the water that formed it, pushes up and out of the underground pocket, carrying some of the water with it. When the steam and water rush out, more superheated water turns into steam and ejects the remaining groundwater out to the surface in the 'gush' typical of geysers. As the plume subsides, the process begins again, as groundwater from above accumulates in the pocket and super-heated water from below enters it.

Geysers require very large volumes of water: some eject tens of thousands of gallons in a single eruption; therefore, geyser basins must have an abundant supply from rain and snowmelt. They also need a strong underground heat source to heat the water and the system must be pressure-tight. If the rocks beneath the basin can leak, a geyser cannot form. The seal is provided by silica dissolved from rocks, so the local volcanic rocks must be silica-rich ones, such as rhyolite. Some of the silica contained in these rocks is dissolved in water and, little by little, is deposited, forming a type of opal called geyserite, or siliceous sinter. Sinter deposits form ornate patterns around geyser basins, though the geyserite critical to the formation of a geyser is, of course, deep below ground. Finally, geysers have a special plumbing system: a narrow spot or constriction, usually close to the surface. The water above the constriction acts as a lid, keeping the water below under high pressure. When the geyser erupts, it blows off the lid.

The appearance of geyser eruptions depends on the surface structure. There are two major types of geyser: cone-type and fountain-type. Most of the famous geysers, such as Old Faithful in Yellowstone, are cone-type, characterised by a very narrow opening just below the surface and, often, a geyserite cone above the surface. The narrow opening acts like a nozzle, resulting in a jet of water that can reach great heights. Fountain-type geysers have an open crater at the surface that fills with water before or during an eruption. Since the jet has to rise through the pool of water, the eruption appears less forceful than those of cone-type geysers; more like a spray or fountain. This type of geyser is far more common than the cone-type: most of the smaller geysers in Yellowstone, such as Imperial Geyser and Grand Geyser, are fountain-type, as is the Icelandic Geysir.

The duration of a geyser's eruption mostly depends on how large its plumbing system is. Most geysers erupt for minutes but a few last for days. The eruption stops either when the geyser runs out of water and goes into a steam phase or, more commonly, because it runs out of heat, in which case the water drains back and the eruption shuts off quickly. Since a geyser's eruption uses up all of the heat and/or water, the geyser has to rest and recover between eruptions; a time of repose called the 'interval'. As the geyser refills, reheats and gets ready to erupt again, it may give some signs, such as bubbling and small splashes, technically called 'pre-play'. This is a good indication of how close a geyser is to its next eruption. Geysers eventually age and shut off; their lifetimes vary but some are active for thousands of years. The silica essential to the formation of geysers is ultimately responsible for their demise, as more and more accumulated silica eventually clogs the fissure.

Yellowstone

Yellowstone, the USA's first National Park, established in 1872, is the most-visited geothermal area in the world. It is also the world's largest caldera (seventy by forty kilometres) and potentially one of its most deadly volcanoes. Yellowstone was designated a Biosphere Reserve in 1976 and a World Heritage Site in 1978.

Plate 1 Active pahoehoe lava flow on Kilauea volcano, Hawaii. (Photograph courtesy of Scott Rowland.)

Plate 2 Active aa lava flow on Kilauea volcano, Hawaii. (Photograph courtesy of Scott Rowland.)

Plate 3 Lava tube on Kilauea volcano, Hawaii. A volcanologist stands by a 'skylight', formed when a portion of the tube collapsed, exposing hot material underneath. (Photograph by Scott Rowland.)

Plate 4 Fire fountain from the Pu'u O'o eruption of Kilauea volcano, Hawaii. Fire fountains are one of the most spectacular products of volcanic eruptions. (Photograph by Scott Rowland.)

Plate 5 The Eldfell eruption in Heimaey, Iceland. The volcano erupted very close to residential areas. (Photograph courtesy of Ralph B White.)

Plate 6 A *nuée ardente* (pyroclastic flow) comes down the Tar River Valley in the Soufrière Hills volcano, Montserrat. (Photograph by the author.)

Plate 7 Contemporary photograph of the devastation of St Pierre, Martinique, from the 1902 eruption of Mt. Pelée. (Photograph courtesy of the US Geological Survey.)

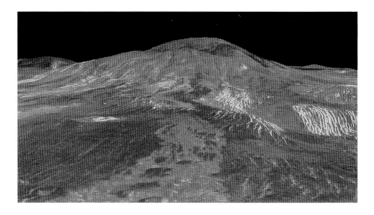

Plate 8 Sif Mons, Venus, is seen in a computer-generated view using images and altimetry data from the *Magellan* spacecraft. The colour is simulated and based on information from the Soviet *Venera 13* and *14* spacecraft. Sif Mons is about 360 kilometres in diameter and 7.5 kilometres high. The image has been vertically exaggerated to show detail. (NASA image.)

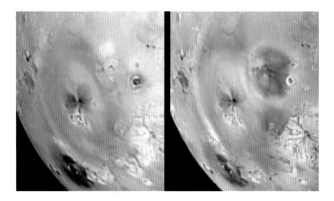

Plate 9 Before and after images of the Pillan eruption on Jupiter's moon Io. The large red oval deposit is from a plume from the Pele volcano. Pillan is located on the north-eastern part of the red deposit. The image on the left was taken in April 1997, before a major eruption that left a 'black eye', seen on the right-hand image, which was taken in September 1997. The dark deposit is thought to be pyroclastics. (Images obtained by the *Galileo* spacecraft.)

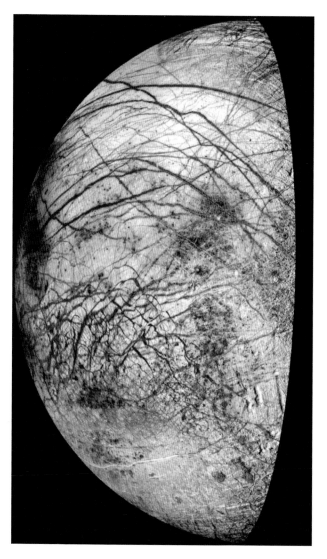

Plate 10 Jupiter's moon Europa has a young surface cut by fractures. Europa harbours a liquid water ocean under its icy crust. It is thought that aqueous mixtures from the interior have erupted onto the surface. (Image obtained by the *Galileo* spacecraft.)

Plate 11 Plumes erupt from Saturn's moon Enceladus. The plumes are mostly composed of water vapour. Enceladus is only 504 kilometres in diameter but its south polar region fractures are the source of large plumes. (Image obtained by the *Cassini* spacecraft.)

It is an outstanding example of a long-lived, large-volume volcanic system caused by a hot spot underneath a continental plate. The current manifestations of its volcanism – its geysers and hot springs – make this area one of the most spectacular volcanic settings in the world.

Yellowstone is a relatively young volcano; all the lavas have been erupted during the last 2.5 million years. The eruptions have been enormous – Yellowstone has erupted some 6,000 cubic kilometres of magma – though this is only a small fraction of the enormous volume of magma that has been intruded under the crust. The eruptions produced gigantic ashflows and three nested, collapsed calderas, the youngest of which is the Yellowstone caldera. The caldera is subtle in its topography, because it is filled by voluminous flows of younger, rhyolitic lavas. Yellowstone has been called a 'supervolcano' in the media and, indeed, it has the potential to unleash catastrophic eruptions. However, the last truly large eruption occurred about 600,000 years ago and it is by no means certain that an eruption of that magnitude will happen again.

Although there have been no magmatic eruptions for some 70,000 years, ground deformation has continued, indicating movement of magma underneath the caldera. The caldera floor was lifted about a metre between 1923 and 1984; since the mid-1980s the floor has subsided at up to 1.5 centimetres a year. There are many other signs that magma still underlies the caldera relatively close to the surface, such as swarms of small, shallow earthquakes and, most obviously, Yellowstone's hydrothermal system, the world's largest, which produces so much heat that the heat flow from the Yellowstone caldera is forty times greater than the Earth's average.

There are more than 400 geysers within the Yellowstone National Park, about two-thirds of the world's known geysers. The Park has nearly 9,000 square kilometres of steaming geysers, hot springs and mud pots, as well as gorgeous scenery and lakes, waterfalls and plenty of wildlife. Visitors to Yellowstone are lucky;

NON-VOLCANIC HAZARDS IN YELLOWSTONE

Yellowstone is still a true wilderness despite its fame as a family holiday destination. Bison are common and wander about freely, sometimes goring tourists who get too close. Bears, including grizzlies, are a major concern for hikers. Magnificent elk roam about and visitors may also see wolves, moose, lynx, bighorn sheep and bobcats. Some deaths in Yellowstone have been tragic but could have been easily avoided, such as that of the young man who decided to scuba dive in one of the hot pools.

they can be sure to see geysers erupt many times every day, making this an ideal place for understanding how they work. Old Faithful, the best-studied geyser in the world, as well as the most famous, is only some 300 years old, so it will delight tourists for many years to come. On average, Old Faithful blows its top every seventy-nine minutes but the interval time ranges from forty-five to 105 minutes, depending on the amount of water left in the system after it has run out of steam.

In 1984, a team of scientists started a detailed investigation of Old Faithful. They measured temperature and pressure every five seconds at eight different depths along the upper 21.7 metres of the geyser throat, its only accessible portion. When they couldn't quite understand the data, which did not match what they expected from the current theories of geyser behaviour, they decided to see what its inside looked like. This seemed impossible but, by 1992, miniature video cameras had become available and they were able to lower a small, insulated camera into the vent, which turned out to have a much more complicated shape than they expected. The video camera showed that the vent was not a smooth pipe but rather a crack running east-west that reached at least 14.3 metres in depth. Some parts of the crack were so wide that the camera (which had a 1.8 metre field of view) could not see the walls; others were extremely narrow – in one place the walls were only fifteen centimetres apart. The camera also showed the walls to be riddled with cracks and that water enters the system continuously at several different depths.

When the researchers put together the map of the geyser's insides with measurements of temperature and pressure, it became clear that the narrow opening plays a critical role, limiting the geyser's discharge rate. For the first twenty to thirty seconds of each three to five minute eruption, steam and boiling water shoot through the narrow gap at the speed of sound. Once the pressure driving the eruption falls below a certain value, the eruption slows down and the geyser begins to shrink. Although these results were ground-breaking, the detailed behaviour of Old Faithful is still not completely understood. The researchers observed that, at times, for several minutes the water in the fissure receded to deeper levels than their equipment could observe, despite the fact that ground-water constantly replaces the water in the fissure. What is really going on at the deeper levels of Old Faithful remains a mystery.

Geysir and Strokkur, Iceland

Some of the most breathtaking manifestations of Iceland's volcanism are its geysers, which lie within a geothermal area containing numerous steaming vents and mud pots. The most famous is Geysir, whose first documented eruption was in 1294 and after which the phenomenon is named. Geysir eventually became one of Iceland's major tourist attractions but, sadly, in the early part of the twentieth century, the eruptions became infrequent and by 1916 had all but ceased. This is thought to have happened because the surface area of Geysir's bowl became much larger so that the water cooled very quickly as it came to the surface.

Eruptions used to be induced at Geysir by various methods: tourists in the early part of the twentieth century poured gravel

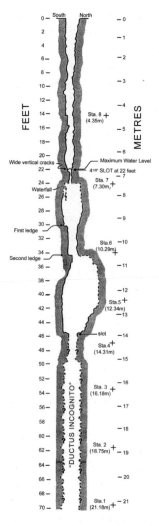

Figure 6 Inside Old Faithful: this diagram shows the upper 14.3 metres of the interior of the geyser. (Modified from a drawing by the late J Westphal who, with his colleague S W Kieffer, used a video camera to probe the inside of the geyser.)

into the bowl to lower the water level and force an eruption. Another favourite method was to pour soap into the water, which decreases the surface tension and facilitates the super-heating of the water, leading to an eruption. Icelanders occasionally used soap to induce an eruption on special days, such as Independence Day. Changes in the activity of Geysir and the less famous geysers in the same area are strongly related to earthquake activity. An earthquake in 2000 put some life back into Geysir but since 2003 its eruptions have again become more infrequent. If it does erupt, it can reach sixty metres in height. Luckily, Geysir's neighbour Strokkur ('the churn') performs reliably every five minutes or so. Strokkur's jet reaches about twenty metres; though impressive, it is over quickly.

Rotorua, Taupo Volcanic Zone, New Zealand

The Rotorua caldera is located within the Taupo Volcanic Zone, potentially one of the most dangerous volcanic areas in the world. The Taupo Volcanic Zone is twenty to eighty kilometres wide and extends from Ruapehu in the south to the Okataina Volcanic Centre in the north and from there continues some 200 kilometres offshore. The 186 CE eruption at Taupo is considered the most violent and explosive known; about 9 cubic kilometres of pumice was erupted and the eruption column heights reached forty-five to fifty kilometres.

The Rotorua caldera was formed during an eruption about 220,000 years ago, which deposited the Mamaku ignimbrite that covered an area of about 2,000 square kilometres. The caldera is about twenty-two kilometres in diameter and now contains a lake with a central rhyolite dome, Mokoia Island. After the caldera collapse, activity has been restricted to the extrusion of three lava domes, with no major explosive activity. In the city of Rotorua, which lies at the south end of the caldera lake, mud pools bubble, steam seeps through cracks and there are geysers in its suburbs. One suburb, Whakarewarewa, has some 500 hot springs and at least sixty-five geyser vents, each with their own name. Seven geysers are currently active: the most famous, Pohutu ('big splash' or 'explosion'), can erupt up to thirty metres, some fifteen times a day. Pohutu, along with its neighbours, Prince of Wales' Feathers Geyser, Te Horu (cauldron) Geyser and Waikorohihi Geyser lie on a sinter plateau about six metres above the Puarenga Stream.

Whakarewarewa was a Maori stronghold; they took advantage of the geothermal activity for warmth and cooking. Many of the thermal features at Whakarewarewa were adversely affected by inhabitants drilling shallow wells to extract hot water for domestic and commercial heating. A bore closure programme between 1987 and 1988 resulted in the closure of 106 wells within 1.5 kilometres of Pohutu Geyser and more than a hundred others beyond there. There has been a pronounced recovery in the activity of the geysers and hot springs at Whakarewarewa.

9
Exotic volcanic activity

The Earth exhibits other forms of volcanic activity that are not so commonly or easily seen. Most of Earth's volcanoes lie underwater; to see them, one needs a submersible. The interaction of magma and water also happens, but differently, in hydromagmatic eruptions, glacier bursts and mud volcanism. There are also some oddball types of volcanic activity, such as carbonatite volcanism.

Submarine volcanism

Most of what we know about volcanoes is based on the 600 or so active volcanoes on land but there are many more underwater, quietly erupting beneath the ocean's surface. We don't know exactly how many, as the deep sea is still a largely unexplored domain. We also don't know exactly how they behave, although in recent years research submersibles have revealed much about the nature of deep-sea volcanic activity, including the appearance of their vents and lavas.

Submarine volcanoes come up at mid-ocean ridges and sometimes create islands, such as those along the Mid-Atlantic Ridge. Mid-ocean ridges are classified into three types: slow, intermediate and fast, depending on the rate of spreading, which can vary from less than two centimetres to more than ten centimetres per year. The volcanic behaviour of a mid-ocean ridge can be directly related to the spreading rate but they have some things in common. First, all mid-ocean ridges erupt almost exclusively basaltic magma (andesite has been found on the Galapagos Ridge but it is extremely rare in mid-ocean ridge environments). Second, all mid-ocean ridges are higher than the surrounding terrain. How much higher depends on the spreading rate but all ridges are like mountain chains in the bottom of the ocean. Third, a valley, trough or depression is commonly found in the middle of the ridge. At slow-spreading ridges, there is a limited supply of magma in the short term but the stress caused by the plates moving apart is constant; therefore, lots of faults form and eventually the magma builds up enough to produce a high-volume eruption. In contrast, fast-spreading ridges have an abundant magma supply, so the constant tectonic stresses cause cracks in the lid of the magma chamber that allow the magma to erupt frequently.

The Mid-Atlantic Ridge is a slow-spreading ridge (less than two centimetres a year). The ridge valley floor has large shield volcanoes, which tend to be elongated, because they are erupted from long fissures on the rift valley floor, formed by the stresses of the diverging tectonic plates. These volcanoes can be as long as five kilometres and as high as two kilometres. Lavas erupted at slow-spreading ridges tend to be pillow basalts, rounded, relatively small extrusions, similar to those erupted at shallow depths. Although eruptions have not been directly observed, scientists have inferred that they are very infrequent, perhaps one every 1,000 to 10,000 years per kilometre of ridge. The eruptions are probably long-lived and erupt large volumes of magma (of the order of a hundred million to ten billion cubic metres).

Intermediate spreading ridges have spreading rates of about six to nine centimetres a year. They are the best-studied type of ridge, mostly because the Juan de Fuca and Gorda Ridges are located just a few hundred kilometres from the north-western coast of the USA, which means they can quickly be reached by ship and instruments placed there which transmit data in real time. The study of these intermediate spreading ridges helps us understand the other two types, as they share some characteristics: some regions of the Juan de Fuca Ridge are very similar to the slow-spreading Mid-Atlantic Ridge, but elsewhere it looks very similar to the fast-spreading East Pacific Rise. Eruption volumes at the intermediate spreading ridges are about one hundred million to a billion cubic metres. Data suggest there is an eruption every five to ten years per kilometre of ridge, lasting between days and weeks.

The East Pacific Rise, near 10°N, a fast-spreading ridge, spreads at about nine to eleven centimetres a year. This ridge is characterised by a broad (five- to ten-kilometre), low (less than 200-metre) rise, topped in most places by an axial summit collapse trough forty to 200 metres wide and six to twenty metres deep. In the Mid-Atlantic Ridge, the trough is formed by tectonic forces pulling the plates apart but East Pacific Rise axial summit collapse trough is formed by near-surface processes; repeated, frequent, small-volume volcanic eruptions, the subsequent draining-back of the lava into the fissure and the collapse of the overlying lava crust. Eruptions in the East Pacific Rise are much more frequent than the ones in the Mid-Atlantic Ridge (on average about one every five years per kilometre) and so are better studied. The eruptions are short-lived, sometimes lasting only a few hours, and produce low volumes of magma, about a million cubic metres. The high spreading rate puts the brittle lid above the magma under constant stress and it cracks frequently. Studies of the East Pacific Rise suggest that there is a ready supply of magma near the surface, waiting to erupt. The magma chamber is long (ten to twenty kilometres), narrow (less than two kilometres) and shallow (ten to a hundred metres deep). The magma appears to be continuously replenished from sources deeper in the mantle, meaning the chamber is almost constantly over-pressurised. When the brittle lid cracks, the magma quickly erupts and relieves the pressure. Once the eruption ends, another doesn't start until the chamber refills; once the chamber is re-pressurised, a small tectonic crack can become a conduit for the next eruption.

Submarine volcanism also occurs elsewhere, such as over the Hawaiian hot spot. Presently, a new volcano, Loihi, is being formed about thirty-four kilometres off the south-eastern coast of Hawaii Island. Loihi currently rises some 3,000 metres above the ocean floor and is 969 metres beneath the ocean surface. Although it will take a long time for Loihi to become Hawaii's newest volcano, it is already intensely monitored and studied, as its location makes it an ideal laboratory for studying the development of an underwater volcano. One day – between 10,000 and 100,000 years' time – Loihi will emerge as a new island in the Hawaiian archipelago.

Hydrothermal vents, a natural part of the interaction of ocean water with hot magma and/or rocks, are found on all the mid-ocean ridges studied to date. The mantle is very close to the ocean floor at mid-ocean ridges; magmas at temperatures of about 1,200°C lurk only a few hundred metres below a spreading ridge. Ocean water percolates down through holes and cracks in the oceanic crust and is heated by the hot magma and rocks. The water reaches very high temperatures (more than 540°C) but because of the great pressure of the overlying rock and water it doesn't boil. The hot ocean water rises up through the cracks and holes in the crust, leaching minerals from the rocks as it goes. By the time it reaches the ocean floor, it has cooled a little but may still be as hot as 450°C. When it comes into contact with the cold ocean water, the hot hydrothermal water rapidly chills and the dissolved minerals come out of solution, creating a smoke-like plume of hot, chemical-laden water. The style of venting varies from place to place; the hottest vents are the *black smokers*.

The first photograph of a black smoker was taken in 1979 by the crew of the submarine *Alvin*. This vent was located about 2.5 kilometres beneath the surface on a ridge off the Mexican coast. *Alvin* literally bumped into what looked like a smoking chimney, breaking off a piece of the column; the pilot,

Dudley Foster, tried to measure the temperature of the vent using the submarine's plastic temperature probe but it quickly began to melt. The instrument could only withstand temperatures up to 330°C, slightly below that of the smoking chimney.

Subsequent explorations have uncovered the amazing volcanic world of black smokers and the cooler vents (with water temperatures of about 20–25°C) dubbed *white smokers*. Their discovery has had a profound effect on our understanding of marine biology and of how life developed on Earth. Black and white smokers are entire ecosystems which survive in the complete absence of sunlight. Basalts contain large amounts of dissolved sulphur, which is leached out and carried up by the hydrothermal waters. Some strains of bacteria, including the ancient and primitive *archeobacteria*, are able to produce energy by combining the sulphur and methane in the process of *chemosynthesis*. These bacteria, in turn, are food for more complex life forms, such as clams, crabs, tubeworms, barnacles and other marine life.

The discovery of these astonishing ecosystems has led many scientists to think that life on Earth may have originated in the deep oceans, around such hydrothermal vents. This has important implications for the likelihood of finding life on other planets. For example, Jupiter's moon Europa is thought to have an ocean of liquid water beneath an icy crust, with hydrothermal vents deep down in this ocean. If we want to look for life elsewhere, Europa's deep ocean is a good place to start.

Hydromagmatic eruptions

When large quantities of hot magma and water come into contact with each other, the results can be highly explosive. The heat of the magma turns the water to steam, which expands explosively, tearing the magma apart and producing great quantities of ash. Magma can also heat up nearby groundwater until the water flashes to steam, resulting in a violent blast. The eruptions can occur within crater lakes, under ice or snow and in shallow water at sea. They are generally referred to as hydromagmatic, hydrovolcanic or phreatomagmatic eruptions (from the Greek 'phreato', well).

Some of the most dangerous hydromagmatic eruptions involve an interaction between magma and ice or snow. The effects can be devastating; the hot magma can melt large quantities of the frozen water, which then rushes downhill, mixing with ash and debris to produce mudflows. Sometimes, however, hydromagmatic eruptions can be relatively contained. For several years during the 1970s, the Poas volcano in Costa Rica delighted tourists with small eruptions from under the murky waters of its shallow crater lake. The explosions shot plumes of the lake's muddy and acidic water into the air, sometimes spraying the tourists who gathered at the crater rim to watch. Though the steady eruptions no longer happen, the crater lake at Poas is still fuming; small eruptions of mud and sulphur are occasionally seen by a lucky few.

Hydromagmatic eruptions can create a type of flow that is exceptionally common in Iceland, when eruptions under glaciers release huge quantities of water. Icelanders term them *jökulhlaup* (*jökul* means 'ice-cap' and *hlaup* means 'deluge') but they are more widely termed *glacier bursts*. The Grímsvötn volcano in Iceland has released glacier bursts with rates approaching 40,000 cubic metres per second, larger than most rivers on Earth. Luckily, these glacier bursts mostly affect uninhabited areas along Iceland's southern coast: one wonders if the volcano-wise people of Iceland deliberately chose not to settle there.

The Icelandic island of Surtsey, which emerged from the sea in 1963, is a superb example of an underwater volcanic eruption creating new land. Surtsey's formation was a hard-to-duplicate spectacle. On 14 November 1963, local fishermen out at sea saw a dark column of smoke, which they thought might be a ship on fire. Luckily, before they got too close for safety, they realised their mistake, as they saw tall jets of steam and ash rising above the surface of the sea. This is typical behaviour for shallow-water eruptions: powerful explosions rip the magma apart, sending ash and fragments hundreds of metres into the air, in a curious shape known as a 'cock's tail plume'.

SAFE HAVEN

As a totally new island, Surtsey is a natural laboratory for biologists, who have studied the island's gradual colonisation by animal life. The isolated island, off limits to most visitors, is a haven for animals. The first species of bird to nest on the new land were black-backed seagulls in 1970, only three years after the end of the eruption. Since then, dozens of birds have been seen on the island and several regularly nest there. Seals also arrived soon after the eruption; within a few years both common seals and grey seals were using Surtsey as a breeding and basking ground.

Surtsey grew quickly: about a day after the eruption started, the new island projected its ashy head above the surface and by 19 November, the young, elongated land mass was 600 metres long and forty-three metres high. Once above the sea, it changed character, becoming a typical Strombolian eruption. Five months after its birth, Surtsey was a sizeable cone over 150 metres above sea level and 1,700 metres long. The loose ash could have been easily eaten up by the continuously pounding waves; however, in 1964 a lava lake filled the island's crater and soon lava began to flow towards the sea. For about a year, lava flowed out of the crater, covering Surtsey's loose ash slopes and assuring the island's survival. By the time activity stopped in 1967, Surtsey had an area of 2.8 square kilometres.

Mud volcanoes

Mud volcanoes (as they are somewhat misleadingly known) are formations created by extruded liquids, such as hydrocarbons and gases, like methane. Unlike 'real' volcanoes, no magma is extruded, so their temperature is, of course, much lower. The material erupted by mud volcanoes is usually a slurry of fine solids suspended in a liquid, typically water or hydrocarbons. The gas emitted by mud volcanoes is mostly methane, with small amounts of carbon dioxide and nitrogen. Approximately 1,100 mud volcanoes have been identified on land and in shallow water and it is estimated that well over 10,000 exist on continental shelves and in the deep ocean. The largest land mud volcanoes are about ten kilometres in diameter and up to 700 metres in high. Mud volcanoes are often associated with petroleum deposits, subduction zones and orogenic belts (sites of crust deformation).

Mud volcanoes exist in the northern front of the Apennines in Italy, in Sicily and in Romania, close to the Carpathian Mountains. There are mud volcanoes on the shores of the Black Sea and the Caspian Sea, several dozen in Russia, on the Taman Peninsula and more on the Kerch Peninsula of Ukraine. Asia also has mud volcanoes, such as those in the Xinjiang province of China and in South Taiwan, where two were recently active. The island of Baratang in the Indian Ocean has several which were significantly active in 2003.

Some mud volcanoes are created by human activity. In 1979, a drilling accident off the coast of Brunei created a mud volcano: it took twenty relief wells and nearly thirty years to stop the eruption. A recent mud volcano eruption – the Sidoarjo mudflow – happened in East Java in 2006, perhaps triggered by drilling (or possibly by an earthquake). The flow eventually covered about 4.40 square kilometres; it inundated villages, roads, rice fields and factories, displaced 24,000 people and killed fourteen. Mud volcanoes, even though they do not erupt magma, can still be lethal.

Cool 'lava': carbonatite

Some volcanoes have significant amounts of calcium and magnesium carbonates in their magma and are low in silica and iron; the lavas erupted by these volcanoes are called *carbonatites*. Carbonatite lavas have viscosities approaching that of water and erupt at temperatures of 500–600°C, considerably lower than basaltic lavas. They form small flows that usually travel only a few metres from their source. While they are usually not a threat to life, their low viscosity means the flows have been known to erupt rather quickly. Only one volcano on Earth, Ol Doinyo Lengai in Tanzania, currently erupts carbonatite lavas. Located in the Rift Valley, near the border with Kenya, this is one of the most active volcanoes in Africa, although its claim to fame for non-volcanologists is as the location of the 'cradle of life' in the film *Lara Croft: Tomb Raider II*!

The origin of carbonatite lavas is not fully understood; it is possible that the carbonates are present in the original magma but they also may be incorporated by the melting of rocks that the magma passed through on its way to the surface. The fact that only one volcano, in a remote location, erupts these lavas makes studying this type of eruption difficult.

10

Volcanoes on other planets: the terrestrial planets

Volcanism, an important method by which planetary bodies lose heat, is a fundamental planetary process that has affected every solid planet in the solar system and many of their moons. Early in the history of the solar system, Mercury, Venus and Mars – as well as the Earth and its Moon – went through a phase of extensive volcanism, when volcanoes brought heat and magma to the surface of the planets: the surface of our Moon was once aglow with vast seas of lavas.

The terrestrial planets of our solar system – Mercury, Venus, Earth and Mars – are relatively small in size compared to the outer gas giant planets, and have rocky surfaces and interiors. Some of the larger moons of the solar system, including the Earth's Moon, Jupiter's moons Io, Europa, Ganymede and Callisto and Saturn's moon Titan may also be considered in this category, though Io is the only one that currently exhibits magmatic volcanism similar to Earth's.

All the terrestrial planets have surface features consistent with volcanic phenomena, although only the Earth has evidence of active volcanism in historic times. The Moon and Mercury, being significantly smaller bodies than the Earth, have cooled to the point where a thick crust caps any fluid magma that may still be inside. Venus and Mars were volcanically active more recently and may still have some activity, methane degassing and hydrothermal activity may be happening on Mars and some Venusian flows are relatively young. Most of our information on the volcanic histories of the terrestrial planets comes from spacecraft data, particularly data from orbiting spacecraft and the few craft that have landed on Venus, Mars and the Moon. There is also evidence from analyses of samples returned from the Moon and meteorites from the Moon and Mars.

The Moon

The Moon is thought to have been formed when a Mars-sized object collided with the Earth shortly after its formation, around 4.5 billion years ago. The enormous collision left a ring of debris in orbit around the Earth, which eventually aggregated to form the Moon. Many planetary geologists consider that the Moon's crust is the result of the cooling and crystallising of a 'magma ocean'. Some 3.9 billion years ago, it is thought that the inner solar system suffered a period of heavy bombardment by rocky material that had not formed planets. These impacts created large impact basins on the Moon, thinning the crust on the near side (the side that faces the Earth) and thickening the crust on the far side.

Today, the Moon is volcanically dead: its last eruptions happened about a billion years ago. It is easy to see the remnants of ancient volcanism on the Moon – just look up on a clear, moonlit night and you will see the dark patches on the Moon's face that were, some 3.5 billion years ago, vast oceans of molten lava. With a small telescope, it is possible to see that the surface of the Moon has regions of rough, bright deposits (the *terrae* or highlands) and regions of smooth, dark, lower elevation deposits (the *maria*, or seas, thus named because they looked like seas to early observers). The highlands have many impact craters and are mostly older than the maria. Samples brought back by

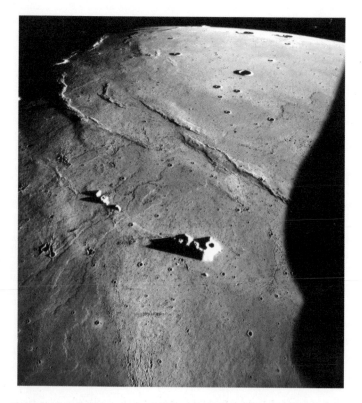

Figure 7 Mare Imbrium on the Moon, showing lava flows on the lower left. The image was taken by *Apollo 15*. The flows can be traced for about 500 kilometres. The dark area on the right is part of the *Apollo 15* spacecraft.

Apollo missions allowed scientists to date the lunar rocks; those of the highlands are very old indeed, at about 4.3 billion years. The maria cover about seventeen per cent of the lunar surface and the older *cryptomaria* cover an additional three per cent. Cryptomaria are ancient (more than 3.8 billion years old) deposits that have been partially buried or covered by highland impact craters or material ejected from impact basins. Basalts, from both lava flows and lava fountains, form a major lunar rock category, with impact breccias and regolith the remaining types. Regolith is fine lunar soil, while *breccias* (fragmented rocks) are formed during impacts.

For many years, the Moon was thought to be very dry but, in 2008, new analyses of Apollo samples, using techniques not available at the time they were brought back, discovered small quantities of water trapped in volcanic rocks and volcanic glass beads (formed when tiny droplets of magma were erupted into cold space and froze, falling to the surface as round, glassy beads). About twenty varieties of these glass beads, which are found in various colours – red, orange and black – are categorised by their chemical composition. The quantities of water are small but these results have changed scientists' view of the Moon and may have important implications for studies of the origin of the Moon and how the inner planets acquired their water.

Even before they could analyse actual rocks, volcanologists knew that the Moon's surface once had lava flows, as their outlines are apparent in places such as the Mare Imbrium. Analysis of rocks from various maria showed that the lavas were very fluid basalts, with varying amounts of iron and titanium. The lunar lava flows were formed by the eruption of large volumes of very fluid

THE NEAR SIDE OF THE MOON

A striking aspect of the lunar maria is that they occur mostly on the lunar near side, the side that faces the Earth. Volcanic eruptions were rare on the far side of the Moon. The Clementine spacecraft in 1994 returned gravity and topographic data that allowed us to understand that the thickness of the lunar crust on the far side is, on average, seventy kilometres, while the thickness on the near side is on average only fifty-five kilometres. Magma rising on the far side was much less likely to be able to erupt through the thicker crust. This difference in crust thickness was a major factor in shaping the lunar surface we see today.

lavas that spread relatively quickly to cover vast areas. Images of the Moon show *sinuous rilles*, winding depressions that resemble river channels on Earth, where lava once flowed. In some places, sinuous rilles are associated with round, pit–like depressions, which probably mark the locations of collapsed lava tubes.

Although the maria, their lava flows and the sinuous rilles are the most common types of volcanic features on the Moon, there

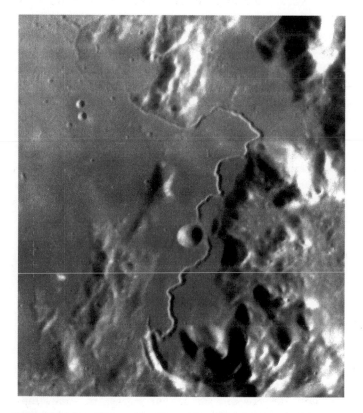

Figure 8 Hadley Rille on the Moon. The rille is about two kilometres wide and 400 metres deep. *Apollo 15* landed close to this location. This image was obtained by the *Lunar Orbiter IV* spacecraft.

also small domes, cones and ash blankets, probably formed by low-volume eruptions from small circular vents or cracks. Lunar cones and domes, such as those found in the Marius Hills region, are steeper than shield volcanoes and were probably formed in short-lived eruptions of alternating lava and ash. They are commonly seen in clusters in the lunar maria and probably mark the locations of vents, which were later covered by younger lavas. Small pyroclastic deposits, probably formed by small explosive eruptions spewing lava fragments and ash, are often found around pits aligned along cracks in crater floors. Other lunar pyroclastic deposits are much larger and tend to be found along the edges of maria. It is possible that they were formed in lava fountains, perhaps similar to Strombolian eruptions on Earth.

What caused some lunar eruptions to be explosive? There are no bodies of water on the Moon's surface, so no interaction of magma and water could have created explosions, and the Moon's magma is basaltic, not the more silicic types that are prone to erupt explosively. Most probably, small pockets of gases (particularly sulphur and carbon monoxide, traces of which are found on the glass beads) propelled the magma into fountains.

Mercury

Mercury, the innermost planet, is still largely unknown: until recently, more than half of the planet was unobserved by spacecraft. NASA's *Mariner 10* spacecraft performed three fly-bys of Mercury in 1973–4, imaging forty-five per cent of the surface. In 2004, NASA launched the *MESSENGER* spacecraft, which will begin orbiting Mercury in March 2011. *MESSENGER* flew by Mercury three times, in January 2008, October 2008 and September 2009; the first and second fly-bys successfully captured images of a further fifty per cent of the surface. Our limited data about the surface of Mercury mean that any conclusions about the abundance and nature of its volcanism are tentative.

Volcanic activity probably ended on Mercury around three billion years ago. Impact craters cover much of Mercury's surface; the *Mariner 10* data showed some smooth plains similar to the lunar maria, with some limited evidence of colour differences, possibly indicating lava flows of different compositions. New insights are coming from *MESSENGER* data, in particular the colour spectral data, which show additional possible volcanic deposits, most likely composed of basalts, and the new high-resolution images have detected a possible shield volcano.

Venus

Venus is a bizarre and hostile place. Surface temperatures are more than 700°C, the atmospheric pressure is ninety times that of Earth and sulphuric acid drizzles from its thick clouds. Venus has plenty of volcanoes – at least ninety per cent of the surface is covered by volcanic materials – but some have no counterpart anywhere else in the solar system.

Venus shows more volcanic terrains and edifices than any of the other terrestrial planets but its thick atmosphere kept its volcanoes largely hidden until the *Magellan* spacecraft, carrying Synthetic Aperture Radar (SAR), mapped most of the planet in the early 1990s. Earlier, in 1982, the Russian *Venera 13* lander imaged a small area around its landing site, revealing a surface that has been interpreted as a lava flow. In the late 1970s, the *Pioneer Venus* spacecraft measured a steady decrease in the amount of sulphur dioxide above the cloud tops. It is possible that a massive volcanic eruption had sent large amounts of sulphur dioxide into the atmosphere and by the time of the *Pioneer* observations, the eruption had ceased and the sulphur dioxide was slowly breaking down. *Magellan* did not find any evidence for surface changes but, more recently, data from the *Venus Express* mission (launched in 2005) identified three lava flows that are different from others in

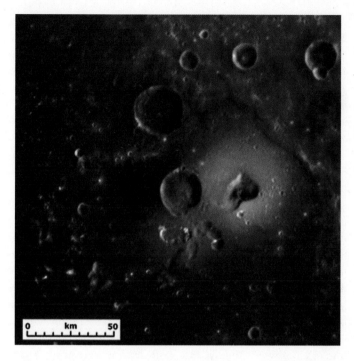

Figure 9 Depression on Mercury's surface (just right of centre) thought to be a volcanic caldera. The image was acquired by the *MESSENGER* spacecraft.

their surface composition. Some interpretations of the data suggest these flows are considerably younger than others, possibly 250,000 years or less old.

The surface of Venus is geologically young, perhaps even active; its relatively small number of impact craters hints at its youthfulness. While it is true that some meteors would burn up in the dense atmosphere or be slowed down enough to be unable to create a large impact crater, it seems this is not the whole story. The craters we see on Venus are either fairly pristine (indicating that they are young) or completely buried (indicating they are old). There are not many in a state of decay somewhere in between. It appears that some major geological event obliterated the craters. One theory proposes that about half a billion years ago, planet-wide and extensive volcanism was triggered after a period of relative quiescence, wiping out many of Venus's impact craters. Then new craters, the ones we see today, began to appear on the surface.

Venus has large plains formed by lava flows, across which run long, sinuous channels, some thousands of kilometres long. The Baltis Valley is the longest lava channel in the solar system, at least 6,400 kilometres long – both ends of this channel have been covered by lava flows, so it is possibly even longer. Although we do not have enough information to be certain of their chemical make-up, the composition of the lavas must be such as to allow them to flow long distances. They may be ultramafic lavas (very fluid lavas, rich in magnesium and low in silica), sulphur-rich lavas or other, more exotic, types. Carbonatite volcanism has also been suggested: carbonatites flow at 490°C, close to the surface temperature on Venus; therefore they would be able to stay molten for long periods. Also, Venus's high atmospheric temperature slows the cooling of lavas, compared to Earth. If flows cool more slowly, they can reach greater distances.

Some of the Venusian volcanoes look similar to those on Earth. There are numbers of shield volcanoes, most less than twenty kilometres in diameter, many clustered into *shield fields*. A few of the shield volcanoes are very large: Sif Mons is about 350 kilometres in diameter and two kilometres high. The large shield volcanoes tend to sit atop broad topographic rises, which suggests they may be over hot spots, similar to the Hawaiian volcanoes. The large volcanoes on Venus have much greater volumes than their terrestrial counterparts, probably because hot spot volcanism on Earth occurs beneath moving plates and a volcano cannot build up in the same place for long periods. In contrast,

Venusian hot spots appear to be randomly located, with no alignments that might suggest the presence of tectonic plates.

Some of Venus's volcanoes look remarkably different from those on Earth and other planets. There are steep-sided but flat-topped domes, nicknamed *pancake domes*, which may be similar to silicic domes on Earth, formed by high-viscosity lava that is extruded slowly, but the Venusian domes, at up to fifty kilometres in diameter, are some ten times larger than Earth's. Another difference is that they have smooth rather than rough surfaces. It is still not clear how the domes formed but they are probably the result of very pasty lava flows slowly extruding and spreading over flat plains. Some pancake domes seem to have given rise to other strange volcanic constructs, for example *ticks*, which appear to be degraded pancake domes. Ticks are radiating ridges that terminate in sharp ends like the legs of a tick; they may be the scars of landslides or could be the result of dykes running from the centre of the dome.

There are also *arachnoids*, volcanic domes surrounded by a cobweb of fractures and crests. Russian scientists named these features after *Venera* radar images showed vast concentric fractures spreading out from volcanic sources, ranging from fifty to 230 kilometres in size. Lines radiating beyond the arachnoids may be

HOW TO NAME A VOLCANO

Volcanoes and other geographical features on planets are named by a committee of the International Astronomical Union. Each planet or moon has its own conventions. Craters on Mercury are named after dead artists, musicians, painters and authors. Venus's features, with the exception of Maxwell Montes, are all female, including goddesses and women's names in various languages. Many names on the Moon and Mars were assigned before the committee was formed, but small craters on Mars, which could not be seen from Earth using telescopes, are now named after small towns and villages around the world.

cracks or ridges resulting from the upwelling of magma stretch-
ing the surface. Another feature is the *anemones*; lava flows
arranged in overlapping 'petals' that extend outward in flower-
like patterns. It is thought that these lava flows occur in association
with fissure eruptions from a series of elongated vents.

Coronae are another feature unique to Venus. They are large
circular or oblong systems of fractures and ridges that span hundreds of kilometres; one, Artemis, is about 1,827 kilometres across.

Figure 10 'Pancake' (flat-topped) domes on Venus. The feature at the
centre of the image is fifty kilometres in diameter; its flat top and steep
sides are typical of 'pancake' domes. It overlies another volcanic feature
that is cut by numerous fractures. Two other 'pancake' domes are seen
to the right and left. This Synthetic Aperture Radar (SAR) image was
acquired by the *Magellan* spacecraft.

Coronae are probably formed by rising blobs or streams of hot material that well up and deform the surface, producing rings of concentric ridges. As the magma pushes up against the crust, the surface rises, forming a dome; then the hot lava spreads out under gravity and flattens. As the area cools, it sinks and cracks, forming a circular ring around a depression. Some coronae appear to be very old and are sunk almost beyond recognition. Most are located along rift systems, where the crust has pulled apart, making it easier for magma to rise up to the surface. Coronae also form at the broad rises of hot spots, in time overlapping with the formation of large shield volcanoes. They often have small shield volcanoes in their interior.

Mars

Mars has the largest shield volcanoes in the solar system, vast plains of lava flows, many lava channels, domes and cones, extensive pyroclastic deposits and considerable evidence of explosive volcanism. Mars has been the focus of planetary exploration since the mid-1990s, visited by orbiters, landers and rovers, so there are vast quantities of data available about the geology of the Martian surface (the composition and nature of the interior has not been well investigated). These data include orbiter and lander images at resolutions ranging from a few centimetres per pixel to several kilometres per pixel and data on surface compositions, atmospheric dynamics and composition.

The first extra-terrestrial volcanic mountain discovered was Olympus Mons, imaged by *Mariner 9* in 1971. When *Mariner 9* arrived, the entire planet was engulfed in a dust storm; when the storm cleared, a dark object appeared in an area named *Nix Olympica* (the 'Snows of Olympus'), a bright area that had been observed by telescope. As the storm further abated, features reminiscent of volcanic calderas in Hawaii began to appear at

Nix Olympica and other nearby mountains. As the mapping of Mars continued over the next eleven months, cartographers re-christened Nix Olympica *Olympus Mons.*

Olympus Mons is the solar system's largest known volcano, standing twenty-four kilometres high, nearly three times as high as Mount Everest. This massive shield volcano's base, 600 kilometres across, would cover the state of Arizona or span the distance between London, UK and Naples, Italy. However, its slopes are gentle, at most 5°. The flanks of Olympus Mons are dominated by tube-fed and channel-fed lava flows, probably basaltic in composition, and its summit has a series of nested calderas more than sixty kilometres across. Olympus Mons has a tall scarp around its base, several kilometres high in places where it has not been covered over by younger lavas. Another peculiarity of Olympus Mons is that it is surrounded by a vast deposit, a terrain consisting of a series of hilly lobes, known as the Olympus Mons aureole material.

While carrying out research on the aureole material, I noticed that the largest deposits were formed adjacent to the areas where the scarp was highest. I proposed that the aureole material had been formed by gigantic landslides that eroded the outer flanks of the volcano and formed the vast, hilly lobes of the aureole. My theory was that the landslides had been triggered by a renewal of volcanic activity in the young Olympus Mons, which caused the permafrost in the volcano's rocks to melt. I'm glad to say that this theory is now well established and accepted by many scientists as the most likely explanation for the aureole's origin. Similar but smaller deposits around neighbouring volcanoes were probably also formed by landslides.

Although volcanic features are ubiquitous across the planet, Martian volcanism is centred on three discrete provinces: Tharsis, Elysium and Circum-Hellas. Olympus Mons is located on a massive rise, the Tharsis Volcanic Province (or Tharsis bulge). Tharsis rises some ten kilometres above the Martian plains and spreads

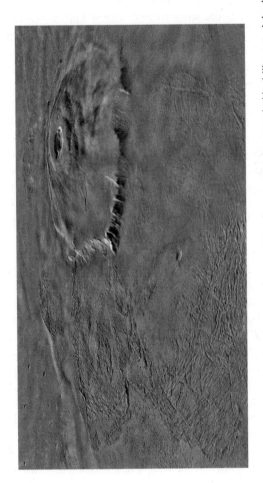

Figure 11 Olympus Mons on Mars, the largest volcano in the solar system, is surrounded by hilly material called the aureole. The volcano is about 600 kilometres in diameter. This image is a combination of Viking images and topography from the MOLA instrument on the *Mars Global Surveyor* spacecraft.

about 8,000 kilometres across, covering twenty-five per cent of the Martian surface. Dozens of volcanic structures dot the region, ranging from tiny cinder cones to volcanoes of the class of – though smaller than – Olympus Mons. Tharsis is home to three other giant shield volcanoes: Arsia, Pavonis and Ascraeus Montes. The summits of these other giants range from fourteen to eighteen kilometres high. There are also several smaller (less than 200 kilometres in diameter) features: the dome-like *tholi*, the *paterae*, irregular or scallop-edged craters, similar to terrestrial calderas, and fields of interconnecting lava plains.

North of Tharsis lies Alba Patera, an ancient, 1,500-kilometre-wide volcanic structure scored by a web of branching valleys and smaller cones and vents that break the surface of the mountain's flanks. It contains two discrete calderas, one over a hundred kilometres in diameter. Alba Patera covers an area larger than Olympus Mons but its slopes are less than 1° and thus it lacks the relief of shield volcanoes. There is some evidence of pyroclastic activity but evidence of lava flows is more common: drained lava channels, collapsed lava tubes and some sheet-like flows. Alba is covered with radial ridges that stay the same width over long distances, typically crested by a channel or series of pits, implying there are sub-surface lava tubes. Superimposed on the lava flows is a net-work of branching valleys; many wander down the flanks showing the same characteristics as water or mud flows on Earth. Thus, Alba not only exhibits many telltale signs of volcanism but also of water erosion. It is not unique in this respect; all Mars's volcanoes have been modified by the activity of water, ice and wind.

The Elysium Volcanic Province, which is about 3,500 kilometres in diameter, is located about 75° west of Tharsis. The province is dominated by three volcanoes and their surrounding lava fields: Elysium Mons, Hecates Tholus and Albor Tholus. Elysium Mons is 500 by 700 kilometres wide and about thirteen kilometres high, making it the fourth-tallest mountain on Mars. This mountain's form is unique: its summit caldera sits atop an asymmetrical circular mountain and to the north, a distinctive two-kilometre-high bench extends for some 200 kilometres. The extension is scoured by flows and sinuous ridges reminiscent of some areas in Tharsis but the main mountain has no such flows; it is covered by hummocky terrain. The entire structure is surrounded by concentric fractures, which may be the scars left after the Elysium volcanoes rose and their weight bore down on

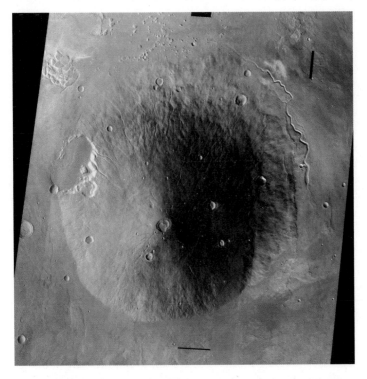

Figure 12 Hecates Tholus on Mars is a steep-sided volcano that is thought to be the result of explosive volcanic activity. The caldera at the top is eleven kilometres across. Image from the *Mars Odyssey* spacecraft (courtesy of Tim Parker).

the Martian crust until it cracked. Hecates Tholus is a different type of volcano; a prime example of a steep-sided volcano thought to have been formed by explosive activity. This mountain, about 160 by 175 kilometres wide and about six kilometres high, whose summit is crowned by a complex caldera eleven kilometres across, has flanks that are heavily scored by shallow linear radial valleys, thought to be water channels formed when the heat from underground magma sources melted surface ice. Since Hecates is so heavily cut into, it may be composed of ash or other easily eroded pyroclastic deposits, whereas Elysium Mons and the Tharsis shields appear to be composed of effusive flows.

The Circum-Hellas Volcanic Province covers more than 4.9 million square kilometres of the Martian surface. It is dominated by patches of volcanoes and their associated flow fields that surround the Hellas impact basin, the largest identifiable impact basin on Mars, spanning 2,100 kilometres. Within this basin are found the remnants of the planet's most ancient volcanoes: the low shield-like edifices of Tyrrhena Patera, Hadriaca Patera and Amphitrites Patera. These volcanoes' heavily channelled and deeply cut shields suggest they are composed of easily eroded pyroclastic deposits rather than lava flows.

The composition of Mars's volcanic features has been assessed by measurements made from Earth, from spacecraft orbiting Mars and from the landers, including the Mars Exploration Rovers *Spirit* and *Opportunity*, which have reached its surface. Visible and near-infra-red spectroscopy, thermal infra-red spectroscopy and *in situ* measurements of volcanic rocks and soils have helped determine the composition of various parts of the surface. No samples collected from Mars have yet been returned to Earth but we can study Martian meteorites that have landed here.

Studies show that most of Mars's volcanic deposits are mafic, similar to terrestrial basalts and basaltic andesites. Measurements of the basalts of the Gusev Crater by the *Spirit* rover suggest that these lavas are probably high-magnesium basalts. In contrast,

Figure 13 Tyrrhena Patera on Mars is thought to be an ancient and eroded volcanic feature. Note the deep, eroded channels. Image from *Mars Odyssey* spacecraft (courtesy of Tim Parker).

analysis of the rock nicknamed 'Barnacle Bill' at the 1997 NASA *Mars Pathfinder* landing site in Ares Vallis suggested it had a slightly more silicic composition, perhaps like the terrestrial icelandite. Elsewhere on Mars, orbital measurements by the Thermal Emission Imaging System (THEMIS) on NASA's 2001 *Mars Odyssey* orbiter identified outcrops of more silicic composition, probably dacites, in Syrtis Major. Like Earth, Mars appears to have a variety of magma compositions.

Despite the widespread occurrence of volcanic features on Mars, evidence for active Martian volcanism is hard to find, but it is possible that future missions will find signs of very recent – or even current – volcanic activity. The most conclusive evidence for current volcanic activity would be if we observed changes on the surface, such as a new lava flow. Despite years of imaging of the surface of Mars by orbiting spacecraft, no evidence of surface changes caused by volcanic activity has been observed but some evidence for recent volcanism comes from the rare Martian meteorites that have been recovered on Earth. The most recent Mars rocks crystallised out of lavas about 170 million years ago, young in planetary terms, and were blown off the Martian surface by a huge meteor or asteroid roughly three million years ago.

Other possible evidence for recent volcanic activity comes from fissures in the Cerberus region, which seem to have leaked dark material onto the surface. The images of the region, taken by the *Mars Global Surveyor*, are not detailed enough to discriminate between lava flows or mudflows but whichever is the case, the Cerberus canyons have had some kind of recent geologic activity. Portions of the Cerberus fissures began as a series of pits, another indication of volcanic-related formation. It is possible that these fissures may still be active. The most tantalising evidence comes from both Earth-based instruments and the Planetary Fourier Spectrometer on the European Space Agency's *Mars Express* orbiter. These measurements have detected methane in the Martian atmosphere, concentrated in particular locations. These results can be interpreted either as signifying volcanic gas production or biological activity. Future missions, such as the *Mars Science Laboratory*, will answer many of our questions.

11

The exotic volcanoes of the outer solar system

Jupiter's moon, Io

In 1979, the camera on board the *Voyager 1* spacecraft captured images of active plumes erupting on Io, one rising 300 kilometres above the surface. When the spacecraft's infra-red instrument showed increased temperatures in some places (dubbed 'hot spots'), one of which coincided with the location of a plume, there could be no doubt that Io was volcanically active.

Io, Jupiter's innermost moon, is the most volcanically active body in the solar system and the only place other than the Earth with large-scale silicate volcanism. Its volcanism was, at first, hard to understand: Io is about the same size as the Moon and should have cooled and formed a thick crust long ago. However, Io is caught in a strange orbital dance with its massive parent Jupiter and the other three Galilean satellites, particularly Europa and Ganymede (the fourth moon is Callisto). For every two of Io's rotations around Jupiter, Europa makes one; for every two of Europa's, Ganymede makes one, and so on. Jupiter's gravitational pull on Io is so great that it creates a tidal bulge on the crust, similar to the way Earth's Moon creates the ocean tides. Without the other moons, Io's bulge would always face Jupiter; there would be no heating of its interior and no volcanism. However, Europa and Ganymede distort the bulge as they pull it towards them; this friction creates heat, which keeps the interior of Io molten.

The two *Voyager* spacecraft showed several volcanic plumes rising above a bizarre planetary surface. The colours of Io, mostly yellows, reds and oranges, with patches of white and black, are consistent with the colours of sulphur. Sulphur dioxide was detected in one of the plumes, so some scientists thought that Io had sulphur volcanism, which is rare on Earth. Others proposed that sulphur and sulphur dioxide formed only a thin coating on the surface and the lavas were silicate, probably basalts. One of the ways of telling sulphur from silicate lavas is by their eruption temperature. The highest temperature detected by the Voyager infra-red instrument was about 300°C but most temperatures of hot spots were found to be around 100°C, roughly the melting temperature of sulphur. Basalt melts at around 1,000°C but cools quickly once erupted, so there was no way of telling if Io's hot spots were molten sulphur or cooled basalt. Unfortunately, neither *Voyager* carried instruments capable of distinguishing the two; their instruments were not sensitive to the shorter infra-red wavelengths, which are best at detecting high temperatures, so the composition of Io's lavas remained undetermined for some time, until infra-red telescopic observations from Earth detected temperatures of around 700°C – too high for sulphur. By this time, the *Galileo* spacecraft was already on its way, with instrumentation better equipped to measure the temperature of Io's hot spots.

Galileo arrived in December 1995 and observed the Jovian system until 2003, when it plunged into Jupiter. Observations of Io's surface between 1996 and 2001 showed many more active volcanoes than had previously been known. During this time, working with the Near-Infrared Mapping Spectrometer (NIMS), I found seventy-one previously undetected hot spots; others were found by *Galileo's* camera and the long-wavelength Photopolarimeter Radiometer. We now know that Io has at least 174 active volcanoes; *Galileo* did not make high-resolution observations of the whole moon and the resolution was poor on the Jupiter-facing side, so it's likely that many more exist – probably at least 400. Results from the *Galileo* mission substantially advanced our understanding of volcanism on Io, showing that its volcanoes come in a range of sizes and with varying characteristics, such as power, persistency of activity and association with plumes.

Most of Io's volcanoes are caldera-like depressions, referred to as paterae (singular patera, meaning 'saucer-like crater'). Unlike terrestrial volcanoes, Io's volcanoes rarely build large topographic structures such as shields or stratovolcano-like mountains. There are only a few dome-like structures, *tholi*, scattered across Io and even some of these are more shield-like, perhaps formed by basaltic volcanism. The most common type of volcanic feature on Io is the *patera* ('saucer'); although the nature of their origin is still uncertain, it is thought to be similar to terrestrial volcanic calderas. Some paterae have angular shapes that suggest some tectonic activity, indicating they may be structural depressions though which the magma travelled to the surface. At least 400 paterae have been mapped; the average diameter is about forty kilometres but Loki, the largest known patera in the solar system, is over 200 kilometres in diameter. (The largest caldera on Earth, Yellowstone, is approximately seventy by forty kilometres.) The larger sizes of the Ionian features probably reflect the much larger sizes of its magma chambers, which are thought to be relatively shallow.

Io's surface shows some remarkably large lava flows. The largest – indeed, the largest active flow field in the solar system – flows some 300 kilometres from the Amirani volcano. Io's large lava flows are possibly similar to continental flood basalt lavas on Earth. Repeated imaging of Amirani during the *Galileo* fly-bys allowed effusion rates to be estimated; at around fifty to 500 cubic metres a second, they are modest by terrestrial flood basalt standards. The ability of the Amirani lava flow field to travel large distances from moderate effusion rates suggests not only that its lavas have a low viscosity but also that they are pahoehoe-like flows, in which the cooled crust insulates the hot material underneath.

Figure 14 Loki Patera, the dark-floored caldera in the centre of the image, is thought to be a caldera on Io containing a lava lake. The caldera is about 200 kilometres in diameter. Active or recently active lavas appear dark. In the centre of the caldera is an island that appears lighter, as it is cold and covered by sulphur dioxide frost. Image from the *Voyager* spacecraft.

Thermal profiles along the Amirani and Prometheus flow fields, obtained using NIMS and high-resolution camera images, suggest these large flows are indeed similar to terrestrial pahoehoe flows.

A major question in Ionian volcanism was whether sulphur or silicates were predominant. Although temperature measurements from *Galileo* clearly showed that many hot spots had temperatures far too high for sulphur, the possibility that some sulphur flows occurred on the surface could not be ruled out. *Galileo* observations showed some locations that may have been sulphur flows: while most Ionian flows appear dark, a few locations showed pale yellow or white flows that could have been molten sulphur. It is possible that rising silicate magma may melt sulphur-rich rock as it nears the surface, producing secondary sulphur flows (as opposed to primary flows that originate from molten magmas at depth). A small sulphur flow of this type happened in Mauna Loa, Hawaii, around 1950. So far, the presence of sulphur flows on Io remains an open question, but the high temperatures detected make it clear that most of the volcanism is silicate.

Most of Io's surface is covered by sulphur dioxide frost, condensed from the volcanic plumes (which are mostly composed of sulphur and sulphur dioxide gas, with a small percentage of silicate ash). Inferring the composition of Io's lavas has been problematic, as no high-resolution spectroscopic measurements could be made. Although the *Galileo* scientists intended to take such measurements, using NIMS, when the spacecraft got close enough to Io to observe the relatively small areas not covered by sulphur dioxide the instrument malfunctioned. With no direct measurements of lava composition available, the temperatures detected at active hot spots provide the best clues to magma composition.

These temperatures can be calculated from measurements made by two instruments, the Solid-State Imaging System (SSI) and NIMS, using wavelength ranges from one to five microns. However, even this is problematic, because of the rapid cooling of lava and the fact that the spatial resolution was of the order of kilometres. The temperature that characterises the composition of the lava is the temperature at which it melts, yet most of the measurements are dominated by cooled lavas, because the red-hot areas are small relative to the size of the pixels. Therefore, the temperatures have to be considered minimum values: we can only say that they are too hot for sulphur and too hot for some types of magma such as dacite and rhyolite. A puzzle soon arose: in 1997, Io's volcano Pillan had a large and violent eruption that created a major change (nicknamed 'the black eye') on the surface. Initial measurements showed temperatures of about 1,500°C – too high for basalt; basalts on Earth rarely exceed 1,200°C.

Recent analysis of the observations of Pillan put the temperature lower, at around 1,300°C, still unusually high for basalts.

Are all Ionian lavas as hot as Pillan's? What are their compositions: are they mafic or ultramafic? We do not yet know whether all lavas on Io are erupted at very high temperatures; it is difficult to detect sufficiently large areas where very fresh (and therefore very hot) materials are exposed. Two main hypotheses have been suggested: ultramafic volcanism and superheated basaltic volcanism. Ultramafic lavas, such as magnesium-rich komatiites, erupted on Earth billions of years ago; if the lavas on Io are of similar composition, we could be seeing a style of volcanism similar to that of Earth's distant past. Alternatively, magmas can be superheated by a rapid ascent from a deep, high-pressure source. The melting temperatures of dry silicate rock increase with pressure; therefore, the erupted lava can be significantly hotter than its melting temperature at surface pressure; rapid ascent of basaltic magmas, resulting in around 100°C of superheating, should be possible. However, no record of such an eruption is known on Earth and most scientists consider the superheating explanation problematic: if the ascent of the magma is slow, it will lose heat through the walls of the conduit. At present, the question of whether Io's lavas are mafic or ultramafic remains open.

There may be other, more exotic but cooler, lavas on Io. One possible magma composition, although rare, is sulphur dioxide. When *Galileo* made repeated close fly-bys of Io, NIMS, though handicapped, was able to map sulphur dioxide distribution. These results showed a nearly pure sulphur dioxide region confined within the Baldur caldera. The sulphur dioxide could have been a liquid flow rising from the sub-surface; although such liquid would normally boil when exposed to the near-vacuum of Io's atmosphere, it is possible that, given sufficiently large quantities, some could freeze to form a layer of sulphur dioxide ice inside the caldera. So far, only a couple of locations have been found where sulphur dioxide may have erupted in this way.

Cryovolcanism

Cryovolcanism is essentially the eruption of materials that would be frozen solid at the normal surface temperature of the icy bodies of the outer solar system; liquid or gaseous water, sometimes mixed with solid fragments. With the notable exception of Io, water is the most important constituent of the icy satellites of Jupiter, Saturn, Uranus and Neptune. While many of the frozen surfaces of these satellites are covered with impact craters, there are some apparently young, smooth areas. These areas are thought to have been resurfaced by cryovolcanism, though it is possible that other processes, such as ice tectonism, diapirism (the convection of solid ice) and intrusive volcanism (in which the 'magma' doesn't break through to the surface) play a part.

For cryovolcanism to happen, the moon must have liquid water in its interior that is able to come to the surface to erupt. A number of factors are important, including the moon's size, the amount of radioactively generated heating and whether the moon's orbit creates tidal heating. Another important factor is the composition of the cryomagma: solely liquid water presents a problem: liquid water is denser than ice, making it hard for water to erupt through a solid ice crust. However, cryomagmas are probably not made up of water alone: the presence of other materials, such as ammonia, could lower their melting point and density, making it easier for them to erupt. The exact composition of the cryomagma depends on the distance of the body from the Sun; in other words, what materials condensed from the solar nebula at that distance. At the orbit of Jupiter and Saturn, methane and ammonia condensed, so it is likely that these could be present in their moons' cryomagmas. In the further reaches of the solar system, carbon monoxide, carbon dioxide and nitrogen may play a greater role. The viscosity of the cryomagmas influences the landforms they produce. Molten water would simply flood a surface, filling in depressions, but a mixture of water and ammonia would have a viscosity like that of silicate lavas, meaning similar landforms would grace these distant landscapes: flows with tall margins, shield volcanoes and domes.

Europa

Europa and Ganymede both show signs of past cryovolcanic activity and it is thought that Europa may still be active. Both show the effects of tidal heating generated as a result of their orbits around Jupiter and their relative orbits to each other. Tidal heating warms Europa's interior, though to a much lesser extent than Io's, and conventional volcanism may exist at the junction of Europa's silicate core and the ocean; a volcano-rich sea floor could nestle beneath its oceanic crust.

Europa's surface is made of nearly pure water ice, with only a few impact craters; the white surface is criss-crossed by linear and arcuate fractures. This indicates it to be very young, by some estimates only about fifty million years old. Researchers have constructed several models to describe conditions beneath Europa's fractured surface, ranging from a thin ice crust with a liquid ocean beneath, to a much thicker crust perhaps up to a hundred kilometres deep. The possible existence of a water ocean beneath Europa's icy crust makes the moon of great interest to planetary scientists. The ocean's presence is suggested by high-resolution images taken by the *Galileo* spacecraft, which showed many fractures across the frozen landscape, bracketed by long ridges rising hundreds of metres. The surface is broken into vast sections of ice called *rafts*, which appear to have shifted and rotated before re-freezing; many can be fitted back together like a jigsaw puzzle, clearly indicating that a once-continuous surface split up and moved around. A second line of evidence that Europa has an ocean underneath its icy crust comes from measurements from *Galileo*'s magnetometer; Europa generates a magnetic field consistent with liquid saltwater.

If surface eruptions do occur, they must be understood in the light of this potential ocean. Europa's orbital stresses and tidal heating make it likely that the ocean floor has volcanic vents. If current models are correct, those vents may be submerged under as much as 120 kilometres of water, deep enough not to disturb the surface, hiding visible clues to Europa's seafloor volcanism. There are dozens of features that hint at forces beneath the crust and past eruptive events involving water that rapidly froze in the near-vacuum of Europa's environment. One is the 'triple bands', parallel stripes that contribute to Europa's cracked appearance. The *Voyager* images showed many stripes, *linea*, seen as bright lines running down the centre of dark, well-defined bands. The bands are less than fifteen kilometres across but run for thousands of kilometres. One, Rhadamanthys Linea, lies across the surface of Europa like a beaded necklace. *Galileo's* imaging system – superior to *Voyager's* – revealed the borders of the bands to be diffuse and irregular in many areas; even the central bright linea displayed patches with halos of bright material spilling across the dark outer band. The triple bands give the appearance of fissures erupting materials onto Europa's bright surface.

A leading theory of how the triple bands form suggests that a tidally induced fault breaks through the ice to the ocean below. A "cryolava" of briny water oozes up to seal the vent, while geyser-like eruptions erupt from weaker locations. These water eruptions coming out of linear fissures may be analogous to fissure eruptions on Hawaii. As the region around the fracture builds vertically, the weight of the growing ridge pulls on the surrounding ice, causing parallel fractures. These cracks, in turn, develop into further parallel ridges as the band expands. An alternative suggestion is that the ridges mark the boundaries of colliding ice plates. These compression ridges sink under their own weight and as the surrounding ice is pulled downward, the sunken troughs along the ridge fill with dark material. While their details are not yet understood, it appears that the ridges may be similar to the mid-Atlantic Ridge.

In some places, mostly near fractures or faults, some material, possibly from geyser-like activity, appears to be staining the ice from beneath the surface; these are known as the *painted terrains*. The stains appear to be volcanic deposits but whether they are local or global in nature is not yet known. In other areas, cryolavas appear to have erupted or seeped onto the surface leaving frozen pools, smooth areas that appear to have enclosed low-lying terrain and oozed into adjacent valleys and troughs before freezing solid.

Europa's most striking cryovolcanic features are the *chaotic terrains*: alongside relatively smooth, craterless landscapes, ridges slip across each other in lateral faults, and remnants of ridged ground have broken and rotated in a slush of debris. Chaotic terrains bear a striking similarity to sea ice in Earth's arctic regions, where solid ice fractures, drifts into new positions and freezes in place again. There is still debate about how these terrains formed but it is thought they are the result of a long and gradual process. Plumes of warm water, generated by ocean floor volcanic sources, could thin the ice, melting, fracturing and freeing rafts of surface ice to float and rotate in the quickly solidifying slush. Another possibility – perhaps more likely because of the probable large distances between Europa's ocean floor and the base of its surface crust – is that the chaotic terrains were generated more indirectly, when hot plumes warmed the ice over a long period, so the heat slowly moved through the ice, much like the waxy blobs in a lava lamp. Gradually, the ice would soften enough to free the rafts. Impurities in the ice, such as small amounts of salt or sulphuric acid (both of which have tentatively been identified by *Galileo*), would help the process by lowering the melting point of water. Yet another possibility is that the ice is heated from beneath without melting through; instead, a rising diapir of ice makes its way through the crust, eventually reaching the surface and possibly interacting on the way with pockets of trapped briny water.

Other possible volcanic features, such as small dome-like features called *lenticulae*, exist on Europa's surface but to really model how these cryovolcanic features form, we need to know the

Figure 15 Conamara Chaos on Europa imaged by the *Galileo* spacecraft. The irregular blocks of water ice were formed by the break-up and movement of the existing crust. The blocks were shifted, rotated and even tipped or partially submerged within a mobile material that was either liquid water or slushy ice. Young fractures cutting through this region indicate that the surface froze again into solid, brittle ice. The area shown in the image is about fifty kilometres across.

thickness of Europa's crust. The next mission to the Jupiter system should answer that question, as it will carry a surface-penetrating radar instrument.

Ganymede

The largest moon in the solar system, with a radius of 2,634 kilometres, Ganymede is larger than Mercury. It has a magnetic field and markedly contrasting geology: dark, heavily cratered terrain forms about one-third of the surface, while the other two-thirds consist of swaths of bright, grooved terrain.

Ganymede's *bright terrain* is almost pure water ice, suggesting cryovolcanism, but it has ridges and valleys, indicating tectonic forces. The bright terrain, sometimes referred to as grooved terrain, is very complex to understand; we don't know its origin with any certainty or why it only covers two-thirds of Ganymede; even with *Galileo*'s high-resolution images, it is still not clear how volcanism and tectonism contributed to its formation. No flows have been identified but there are some arcuate depressions, perhaps similar to volcanic craters or calderas on other planets, which could be the sources of flows and of some of the bright terrain materials. Nor do we know why the bright terrain is located in swaths that criss-cross the moon and why the whole moon was not affected by the resurfacing.

Ganymede is a mysterious world, with much for future researchers to find out. At present, the European Space Agency is planning a mission that will orbit Ganymede, to be launched at around the same time as NASA's mission to Europa.

Titan

Titan, Saturn's largest moon, is one of the most exotic and mysterious bodies of the solar system. It has the second-densest atmosphere of any of the solid bodies, behind Venus. This atmosphere shrouds Titan, completely veiling it. When *Voyager 1* flew by in 1981 it could see nothing beneath the atmosphere, but the *Cassini-Huygens* mission, which reached Titan in 2004, continues to reveal more of its surface detail.

Titan has long been thought to be a likely place for volcanic activity. It is large – at 5,150 kilometres in diameter, larger than Mercury and second only to Ganymede in the moons of the solar system. Titan's substantial mass and density suggest that plenty of gravitational and radioactively generated energy is available for melting its interior. In addition, its eccentric orbit around Saturn provides some tidal friction, though much less than Io's. Various models of Titan's interior suggest it has a substantial layer of water-ammonia liquid lying beneath an icy shell. If there were enough fracturing, the liquid could erupt through

Figure 16 Ganymede, the largest moon in the solar system, showing dark and bright grooved terrain. Image acquired by the *Galileo* spacecraft.

to the surface. Titan's dense atmosphere makes it far harder for gases to emerge from cryomagma and for any explosive products to be thrown far from the vent. It would also cool cryolavas quickly. Therefore, it was thought that Titan would be more likely to have effusive rather than explosive deposits. Laboratory experiments and theoretical work predicted that Titan's cryomagmas were probably a very cold mixture of water and ammonia, possibly with some methanol, and would flow in quite a viscous manner, similar to basalts and basaltic andesites on Earth. Titan's cryoflows could therefore look very much like a lava flow on Earth.

Titan's thick atmosphere is about ninety-five per cent nitrogen, with a few per cent of methane. The methane in Titan's atmosphere is photo-dissociated: sunlight breaks it down so that it recombines with other constituents of the atmosphere, forming organic compounds such as ethane, propane and acetylene. For this process to continue, the methane must somehow be replenished. One thought is that large liquid bodies on the surface (perhaps liquid methane or ethane), maybe even an ocean, could re-supply the atmospheric methane; at Titan's temperatures (−176°C at the surface), methane, behaves much like water on Earth. *Cassini* revealed large bodies of liquid on the surface, perhaps enough to replenish the atmospheric methane, but another possibility is that cryovolcanism supplies methane and other gases to the atmosphere. Titan's atmosphere may have begun as ammonia (NH_3) erupted from the interior in massive events. The ammonia was later converted to nitrogen (N_2) by ultraviolet photolysis and escaped as hydrogen to space.

Cassini results suggest that cryovolcanism has indeed been a significant geological process on Titan. The craft carries a radar instrument that can operate in Synthetic Aperture Radar (SAR) mode, peering through the clouds and haze to the never-before,-seen surface. The *Cassini* SAR showed that several large flows were spread across Titan's frigid landscape; some, particularly those that appear to come out of craters, are likely to be cryovolcanic, though some researchers argue that some of the flows could possibly be fluvial. Titan's surface has fluvial activity, as shown by plenty of branched channels, indicating that rivers of liquid methane run there. Cryovolcanism can also cause flows, so the challenge is to identify which process caused a particular flow deposit. Some of the flows seen in the radar images are more likely to be cryovolcanic than fluvial, particularly those that appear to come out of craters. The craters are elongated rather than circular, indicating origin by collapse (volcanic) rather than by impact. The association of flows (in one direction only) with non-impact craters is hard to explain by any process other than volcanism. Titan may still be actively cryovolcanic: *Cassini*'s Visible and Infra-red Mapping Spectrometer (VIMS) observed periodic brightening at two locations that could not be explained by changes in cloud cover. It is possible that active cryovolcanism, perhaps in the form of degassing, causes the brightness changes. When the radar instrument observed these locations, they showed flow features that could be due to cryovolcanism.

Whether or not Titan is currently actively volcanic, it is likely that it was in the past. The Huygens probe, which landed on Titan on 14 January, 2005, obtained other evidence that cryovolcanism may have occurred on Titan. Although the amazing surface images did not show any features that could be unambiguously interpreted as cryovolcanic, there was a surprising finding by the Gas Chromatograph Mass Spectrometer. This instrument detected the radioactive isotope of Argon (^{40}Ar) in Titan's atmosphere. This isotope is a product of potassium (^{40}K) decay and its presence in the quantities measured means that the atmosphere must be in communication with a reservoir of the parent atom. Titan is large enough to have differentiated, that is, it evolved into compositionally distinct layers, with the denser materials sinking to the centre. Therefore, it is likely that most of the potassium-bearing material is in the silicate rocks that forms Titan's core. Cryovolcanism would be one means by which this material might be brought to the surface. At the time of writing, the *Cassini* mission is still obtaining amazing images of Titan's surface and new clues to its volcanic history may yet be revealed.

Enceladus

Enceladus is located in Saturn's E ring (the rings of Saturn are lettered in the order of their discovery). The discovery of active volcanic plumes on Enceladus was perhaps one of the most exciting of the *Cassini* mission. Despite its small dimensions (252 kilometres), Enceladus's surface appears smooth and young, with few impact craters; it is also very bright, indicating that it has a pristine ice surface

100 km

Figure 17 Bright areas on Titan that may be cryovolcanic flows. The large, lobate deposits are Winia Fluctus, while the small lobate flow to the right is Rohe Fluctus, which appears to come out of a crater. Synthetic Aperture Radar image taken by *Cassini*.

dusted with fresh materials. Suggestions of active cryovolcanism had been made before *Cassini*, when the *Voyager* spacecraft showed some apparently young areas that appeared to have been distorted either by tectonic activity or flows of very viscous materials.

When *Cassini* arrived at Saturn in 2004, its magnetometer started mapping the magnetic field around Saturn and its moons. The results of this mapping showed that ions from Enceladus were causing changes in Saturn's magnetic field. Two fly-bys of Enceladus, made in the first half of 2005, showed ions streaming from Enceladus's southern hemisphere. These results were so exciting that the spacecraft's orbit was changed so that, on 14 July 2005, it flew only 168 kilometres above the surface. The results were incredible: *Cassini* flew through an extended plume of material in which instruments detected water vapour, methane and carbon dioxide. The Composite Infra-Red Spectrometer (CIRS) detected heat over one of the long rifts of the south polar region. *Cassini* images revealed spectacular plumes whose sources coincided with the rifts. These parallel rifts, about two kilometres across and up to 130 kilometres long, nicknamed *tiger stripes*, appear to be the source of volcanic plumes. Most of Enceladus is composed of nearly pure water ice but the tiger stripes show the presence of organic compounds and carbon dioxide: material is coming from the interior to the surface at these locations.

Saturn's E ring is very tenuous and it was thought that it was somehow being replenished, probably by fine particles that came out from Enceladus. The material in the plumes is being ejected at about sixty metres per second; the eruptions could be large enough to be the source of supply for the ring. The plumes may be linked to reservoirs of liquid water beneath the surface; if this is true, Enceladus could be as exciting as Europa as a potential environment for life. Enceladus has an internal heat source, although its origin is unknown. It is possible that tidal heating could be localised in a thermal plume or diapir in the interior of this small moon, leading to partial melting of the icy crust at the south pole.

The northern hemisphere of Enceladus appears to be older; all the cryovolcanic activity detected so far has been seen at the south polar region.

Triton

Voyager 1 discovered active volcanism on Io but *Voyager 2* found volcanic activity in an even more unlikely body: Neptune's small moon, Triton (radius 1,353 kilometres). When *Voyager 2*'s trajectory took it above the south pole on 25 August 1989, Triton became the most distant and coldest moon to be visited by a spacecraft. This was *Voyager 2*'s last 'stop' before it travelled to the outer edges of the solar system and beyond.

When the images were analysed, they showed two dark, tall plumes, reaching about eight kilometres above the surface and leaving trails for about 150 kilometres. Other images of Triton's southern polar region revealed more than a hundred dark, streaky deposits, presumably the result of other plumes, implying that plume activity must be fairly common. This single fly-by could tell us little about cryovolcanism on Triton: for example, the northern polar region was in darkness, so it is not known whether there are active plumes there. At lower latitudes, the images showed a peculiar terrain with flow-like features, dubbed *cantaloupe* because of its resemblance to melon skin, probably resulting from cryovolcanic flooding of older topography. Other features, *guttae*, showed dark centres surrounded by bright materials and are also probably cryovolcanic.

Cryovolcanism on Triton is very different from cryovolcanism on the satellites of Jupiter and Saturn. Triton's surface is extremely cold, −235°C, well below the freezing point of nitrogen, which makes up the south polar cap. Nitrogen and methane have been identified on Triton's surface; carbon monoxide and carbon dioxide have been detected in small amounts. Water ice is likely to be present in the crust but it has not yet been detected. Triton has a very thin atmosphere, largely made up of nitrogen. The atmosphere transports frozen nitrogen from pole to pole

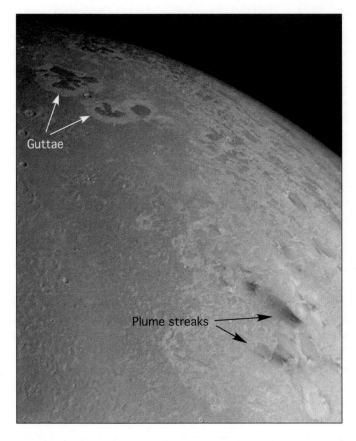

Figure 18 Neptune's moon Triton, imaged by the *Voyager* spacecraft. The guttae are large lobate features, thought to be cryovolcanic. The dark plume streaks can be seen against the bright terrain. The area shown in the image is about 1,500 kilometres across.

every Triton year, keeping the surface temperature nearly the same everywhere.

Triton has a very unusual orbit; it is oblique with respect to Neptune's equator and is retrograde (opposite to Neptune's direction of rotation), which suggests that it did not form near Neptune but, rather, was captured by it. As consequence of this capture, Triton may have undergone large tidal heating and melting of its interior ices. Some surface features, such as the cantaloupe terrain, may have been formed by diapirism, upwelling of material from the interior. Moreover, because of Triton's oblique orbit, the latitude of the subsolar point (the point where the Sun appears to be directly overhead) wanders as far as 55° from the equator. Triton's southern hemisphere was just approaching summer solstice, the Sun beating down on the rarely illuminated south polar region, when *Voyager* flew by; a rare event, as Triton's year lasts 165 Earth years. The active plumes were located close to the subsolar point.

There is no evidence that the flows and other volcanic-looking features on Triton are still active, but what is powering the plumes? The chief hypothesis is that the plumes are similar to geysers, caused by the sublimation of the polar cap (changing from solid directly to gas, without passing through a liquid phase); the result of sunlight hitting the surface and penetrating a transparent layer of frozen nitrogen. Frozen nitrogen is very clear, so sunlight can penetrate deep into it, creating a 'solid-state greenhouse effect'. Sunlight is absorbed and trapped by dark, carbon-rich impurities a few metres below the surface. This mild heating is enough to cause the interior of the frozen nitrogen to turn to gas, because even a small increase of about 10°C over the surface temperature is enough to raise the vapour pressure of nitrogen by a factor of one hundred. The expanding gas then explodes into the near-vacuum of Triton's environment. If this model is correct, active cryovolcanism on Triton is a side-effect of sunlight, rather than an internally driven phenomenon.

Enceladus and Triton have certainly shown that even small moons can have active volcanism. Other icy satellites, such as Ariel, Miranda and Titania (moons of Uranus), have features related to resurfacing and possibly to eruption of material on the surface by cryovolcanism. As we continue to explore the solar system, active volcanism may be found in some surprising places.

12
Volcano research

Volcanoes are extremely complex systems and many studies combine towards the ultimate goal of understanding how they work. Volcanology is a combination of a number of disciplines: geology, physics, chemistry, geography, mathematics and others. The science of volcanology has changed considerably in the last few decades; it used to be reserved for studies of terrestrial volcanoes, in particular, to methods that could be used for eruption prediction and hazard assessment. The Australian engineer, GA M Taylor, called volcanology 'the Cinderella science which only marches forward on the ashes of catastrophe'.

The discovery of extra-terrestrial volcanism has changed this view. Decades ago, almost all volcanologists began as geologists. These days, the importance of mathematical modelling of eruption processes has been recognised and has enabled huge advances in our understanding of eruptions. Some of this change came about because of planetary volcanology: traditionally-trained geologists could not travel to those fields to map and collect samples. Factors such as different gravity, the thickness and composition of a planet's or moon's crust and the presence or absence of an atmosphere are important factors when studying extra-terrestrial volcanoes. Because volcanoes are so complex, many disciplines are needed to work towards the ultimate goal of understanding how they work. For the Earth, this understanding can be put into practice in eruption prediction, often saving thousands of lives.

Surveillance and eruption prediction

The successful forecasting of eruptions, one of the most important goals of volcanology, is not easy to achieve, not only because of the complexity of the processes but also because not all volcanoes behave in exactly the same way. Volcanoes are very individual; some are reasonably predictable, others are not.

To predict a volcano's behaviour, it is very important to know that specific volcano's long-term eruption pattern. Eruptions rarely come unheralded but the critical signs that one is about to happen are not always the same for every volcano. If the volcano is not monitored, these signs may be missed altogether, with tragic results. Eruptions cannot be stopped but much can be done to minimise their death toll and the economic havoc that they cause. Volcanologists strive to understand and interpret the signs of an impending eruption using a wide variety of information, from seismic activity to analysis of gases. Although we are still not able to predict exactly when and where an eruption will happen, we can detect departures from a volcano's normal behaviour that may be precursors. One volcano's eruption precursors might not be those of another, but any volcano about to erupt nearly always exhibits a number of changes in behaviour. The more we know about any particular volcano, and the longer it has been monitored, the greater are our chances of correctly interpreting those warnings.

Monitoring volcanoes involves making frequent measurements of a variety of volcanic phenomena, including earthquakes, ground movement, chemical compositions of the gases emitted by the volcano, changes in the local electrical, magnetic and gravity fields and ground temperature. Most measurements can be made on the volcano but others can be taken from aeroplanes or even by Earth-orbiting satellites. Such remote-sensing techniques enable volcanologists to monitor very isolated or otherwise inaccessible areas where ground monitoring might be expensive or difficult. They are continuously improving our knowledge of the topography, surface changes and thermal activity of some of the Earth's most remote volcanoes. For these inaccessible volcanoes, satellite images may be the first indication that an eruption is taking place and once an eruption starts, satellite data can be very important for monitoring its progress.

The most common techniques involve measuring ground movement, either in the form of earthquakes or inflation of the ground. Typically, when magma moves up towards the surface and is fed into a reservoir, it causes the ground to inflate. One can imagine the magma as a balloon being inflated. The pressure causes the ground to be pushed upwards and outwards and it changes the slope of the ground and the distance between two points on the surface. These effects can be measured by a variety of instruments, as well as by repeated field topographic surveys. The instruments are becoming more and more automated and precise so that even minute changes in ground level can quickly be detected. Seismometers are used to detect magma movement towards the surface, as the inflation of the ground causes fracturing of rock that, in turn, causes earthquakes. A network of seismometers placed on a volcano can easily and accurately provide information on the frequency, location and magnitude of earthquakes. Measurements of seismic activity and ground deformation are generally the most important for volcano monitoring, but they cannot be used by themselves to predict eruptions unless the behaviour of the volcano is fairly well understood by other means. For example, if the magma chamber is deep, ground deformation at the surface may be too small to be a good indicator of magma movement.

Changes in a volcano's geothermal system, the heated waters and fluids that surround the hot magma, can also be precursors of eruptions, because the influx of new magma into the chamber, or movement of magma already there, can cause certain gases or fluids to be released. Signs that can be detected at the surface include variations in the temperature, chemical composition and emission rates of gases and fluids coming out of surface cracks, fumaroles and hot springs. For example, an increase in the amount of sulphur dioxide gas coming out of fumaroles is generally a sign that new magma is moving towards the surface. At present, geochemical monitoring is not as commonly used on volcanoes as ground movement techniques but, as these signs become better understood, this is likely to change. Other techniques rely on geophysical effects, such as deviations in the local gravitational, geomagnetic and geoelectric fields. These changes can reflect changes in the temperature or ratio of the volcano's magma, water, gas and solid rock components.

Planetary studies

The huge leaps forward in remote sensing techniques have not only been useful for Earth: our observations of other worlds have been enormously helped by the development of new instruments. Infra-red spectrometers measure the composition of the surface, long wavelength infra-red spectrometers show which areas are covered with fine particles and which are rock, radar peers below the surface and the optical images become ever more detailed – it is amazing that we can now see the surface of other planets at a resolution of a few metres per pixel.

For reasons of distance, expense and danger, planetary volcanology largely relies on robotic eyes. Landers and rovers are our robotic field geologists: it is easier and cheaper to send a robotic laboratory to a planet than humans to collect samples and bring them back to Earth. Human exploration is an expensive pursuit, not to mention a high-risk one, so robotic spacecraft have brought back samples from the Moon and, in the next decade or so, may bring back samples from Mars, asteroids and comets. There are plans to return humans to the Moon and send them to an asteroid and to Mars but no timetable as yet. When these humans go, they will no doubt collect rock samples and either analyse them in robotic laboratories or bring them to Earth. In any case, the Moon, Mars and some asteroids are the only extra-terrestrial bodies where human exploration is likely to happen, at least for the next few decades. Other bodies, such as Venus and Io, are too hostile for humans; the technologies needed for human survival on their surfaces have not yet been developed.

Understanding the geology of other bodies is also problematic because of scale. On Earth, we can send field geologists to many different volcanoes; on other planets, we must try to understand the geology of a whole body using the glimpses from a few spacecraft or, very rarely, a lander. Therefore, planetary volcanology has to take a global rather than local view: it is more important to understand the volcanic activity of the whole body than the working of one particular volcano. However, there can be no doubt that our knowledge of volcanism as a process has benefited enormously from studies of other planets. Before Io's volcanic activity was discovered, tidal heating was not thought of as a mechanism that could enable a small body to have a molten interior; studies of other planets have shown us that Earth's volcanism is unique in being driven by plate tectonics, a process not detected on any other body in the solar system.

As we increasingly set Earth's volcanoes into a solar system-wide context, we discover both what makes its volcanoes unique and also how taking a planetary rather than an Earth-centric view can expand our knowledge of volcanic processes.

Bibliography

A Field Guide to Yellowstone's Geysers, Hot Springs and Fumaroles. Carl Schreier (1992). Wyoming: Homestead Publishing.

Alien Volcanoes. Rosaly Lopes and Michael Carroll (2008). Foreword by Arthur C Clarke. Boston, MA: John Hopkins University Press.

Encyclopedia of Volcanoes. Edited by H Sigurdsson, B Houghton, SR McNutt, H Rymer and J Stix (2000). Academic Press.

Geysers, What They Are and How They Work. T Scott Bryan (1990). Colorado: Roberts Rinehart.

Inside Old Faithful. S Perkins (1997). *Science News*, 152, October 11, 1997.

Io After Galileo. Edited by R Lopes and JR Spencer (2006) Praxis Publishing Company.

Krakatau 1883: The Volcanic Eruption and Its Effects. T Simkin and RS Fiske (1983). Washington, DC: Smithsonian Institution Press.

Lessons from a Major Eruption: Mount Pinatubo, Philippines. The Pinatubo Volcano Observatory staff (1992).

Earth in Space, for Teachers and Students of Science. American Geophysical Union, February 1992.

Mountains of Fire: The Nature of Volcanoes. Robert and Barbara Decker (1991). Cambridge: Cambridge University Press.

The Volcano Adventure Guide. Rosaly Lopes (2005). Cambridge: Cambridge University Press (Portuguese translation by Oficina do Texto, 2008).

Volcanic Worlds: Exploring the Solar System Volcanoes. Edited by Rosaly Lopes and Tracy Gregg (2004). Foreword by Sally Ride. Praxis Publishing Company.

Volcanism. Hans-Ulrich Schmincke (2003). Springer-Verlag.

Volcanoes of Europe. Alwyn Scarth and Jean-Claude Tanguy (2001). Oxford: Oxford University Press.

Volcanoes of North America: United States and Canada. Edited by CA Wood and J Kienle (1990). Cambridge: Cambridge University Press.

Volcanoes of the Solar System. Charles Frankel (1996). Cambridge: Cambridge University Press.

Volcanoes of the World (2nd edition). Edited by Tom Simkin and Lee Siebert (1994). Geoscience Press in association with the Smithsonian Institution.

Volcanoes, a Planetary Perspective. Peter Francis (1993). Oxford: Oxford University Press.

Volcanoes. Edited by P Francis and C Oppenheimer (2004). Oxford: Oxford University Press.

Volcanoes. Robert I Tilling (1999). US Geological Survey: US Government Printing Office.

Volcanoes: An Introduction. Alwyn Scarth (1994). Texas A&M University Press.

Melting the Earth. Haraldur Sigurdsson (1999). Oxford University Press.

Index